Virgin Atlantic

John Balmforth

MIDLAND

An imprint of
Ian Allan Publishing

CONTENTS

First published 2009

ISBN 978 1 85780 303 7

Published by Midland Publishing

an imprint of Ian Allan Publishing Ltd, Hersham, Surrey, KT12 4RG
Printed in England by Ian Allan Printing Ltd, Hersham, Surrey, KT12 4RG

Code: 0905/B

Visit the Ian Allan Publishing website at www.ianallanpublishing.com

FOREWORD

How 25 years have flown by! I remember that day, 22 June 1984, so vividly. Our first aircraft, a Boeing 747 in Virgin Atlantic colours, on the tarmac at Gatwick Airport waiting for its very excited load – 300 inaugural passengers heading off to Newark, New York. And so VS1 was born.

There were many who said we couldn't do it and that we'd be out of business within weeks. They said that the big boys of the aviation industry would eat us for breakfast. How wrong they were. Twenty-five years on and Virgin Atlantic is flying high. With nearly 40 aircraft in the fleet, and many more on order for the coming years, we are now seen as one of the top three airlines in the world and we have the trophy cabinet to prove it. Several cabinets, in fact, as our people have won so many awards for their innovation, professionalism, customer service and sheer excellence.

Virgin Atlantic continues to set the standards for the rest of the industry. When we set up the airline in 1984, we had one overwhelming objective – to fly the best, not the biggest airline, and I truly believe we have the best service in the skies today. In every cabin, from the incredible fully-flat beds in Upper Class, to the spacious Premium Economy, a cabin we invented and which is now copied by other carriers, to the leading Economy cabin, where we were the first to install video screens at every seat (remember how awful travelling was in the days before those screens), we have sought to create a memorable experience in long-haul travel.

It's not just in the air but on the ground as well that we shine. We have created The Clubhouses, voted as the best lounges in the world, in various destinations – not just at Heathrow or Gatwick. In fact, at every point on the Virgin Atlantic journey, we have listened to our customers to create something special, perhaps even magical. There aren't many companies in the world with whom you would choose to spend time for many hours at the beginning and end of your trip. Yet, in our short history, we've carried over 65 million people around the world.

So, what's in store during the next 25 years? I hope there'll be more of the same. The same innovative streak running through our business, the same high standards that lead the industry and the same focus on employing the best people providing the best experience to our passengers. If you've helped in our success over the last 25 years, then thank you for your belief in us. Here's to many more memories over the next 25.

Sir Richard Branson
President, Virgin Atlantic Airways
May 2009

INTRODUCTION

We have a simple but clear mission at Virgin Atlantic. It's to run an airline that people love to fly and where people love to work.

We fly the same aircraft as our competitors, from the same airports, to many of the same destinations. Yet our passengers keep coming back because we do something different. We inject a complete focus on customer service across the company. It's been the hallmark of Virgin Atlantic since the day that first flight took off for New York and it's served as our company philosophy ever since. Everything we do, day in day out, is geared towards our passengers. They pay for an experience and a high standard of service, so it's up to us to deliver.

Virgin Atlantic doesn't really have a right to exist. No other flag carrier around the world has a major competitor flying long haul. Air France, Lufthansa, Iberia, the list goes on. Not one of them has heavy competition snapping at their heels in the same way that Virgin Atlantic competes against the giant that is British Airways. It is the unique status of Heathrow that enables us to do this.

It is a tribute to the people at Virgin Atlantic that, over its 25-year history, the airline has managed to outwit and often outpace BA. It's certainly a testament to the very philosophy that drives our business – providing the best service.

We've grown from flying one route to flying to 30 destinations around the world. From our UK bases at Heathrow, Gatwick, Manchester and Glasgow we service the world's most important and popular destinations, such as Hong Kong, Tokyo, Sydney, Shanghai, Delhi, Los Angeles, New York, Washington, Miami, Las Vegas, Barbados, Antigua, Kingston, Montego Bay, Orlando, Johannesburg, Cape Town, Dubai and many more.

Our 9,000 staff are rightly proud of our achievements so far. But there's so much more we can do over the next 25 years. With new eco-friendly and fuel-efficient Boeing 787-9 Dreamliners due to be delivered, we'll be able to fly to even more destinations and increase our frequency on existing routes. We'll be able to set even higher standards in the industry with the next generation of in-flight seating and entertainment. Crucially, we'll perhaps be able to fly short haul, as the industry consolidates and refreshes itself for a new era.

But that's all for the next book in 25 years' time. For now, we hope the next few chapters offer you just a small taste of the highlights since 1984, and the enormous fun that we've had creating one of the best airlines in the world.

Steve Ridgway CBE
Chief Executive, Virgin Atlantic Airways
May 2009

▲ *Steve Ridgway CBE, Chief Executive of Virgin Atlantic Airways.*
Virgin Atlantic Airways

▼ *The Virgin Atlantic route map showing destinations served, displayed at the Crawley Training Centre.*
John Balmforth, courtesy of Virgin Atlantic Airways

PREFACE

These days Sir Richard Branson is world renowned as a businessman who will venture into areas where others fear to tread. His name is inexorably linked to the Virgin brand, and both have become well-respected household names. He likes nothing more than to succeed when pitting his wits against the so called 'big boys' with the odds stacked against him, so perhaps it should not have been a surprise when he decided to get involved in running an airline. Certainly the story of Virgin Atlantic Airways underlines this and reveals a fascinating tale of a fledgling airline fighting against the odds to survive the financial difficulties, and what became known as the 'Dirty Tricks Campaign' by British Airways in an attempt to put the Virgin airline out of business.

Richard Branson also loves the physical challenge as epitomised by his many ballooning exploits and the high-speed crossing of the Atlantic Ocean aboard Virgin Atlantic Challenger II which successfully regained the Blue Riband for Great Britain. Many are aware that in both of these activities he came close to losing his life, but perhaps it is not so widely known that arguably his greatest escape came near to his Oxfordshire home in 1977 when he agreed to try out a 'home-made' flying machine.

Richard Ellis had sent the fun-loving Branson a photograph of an invention which he called a 'pterodactyl flying machine'. The picture showed a man on a tricycle which was attached to two large wings, with the machine seemingly flying above the treetops. Ellis's idea was for Branson to try out the machine and buy the licence to distribute it. Totally intrigued, Branson invited Ellis to his home so that he could view the 'pterodactyl'. It was powered by a small outboard motor with rotors fitted above the 'pilot'. Take-off required the 'pilot' to pedal hard along a runway; eventually the motor would cut in and provide power to increase the machine's speed and power the rotor when it became airborne after take-off. Branson recalls Ellis telling him, "It'll take you a couple of weekends to get used to it so you won't take off this time." A rubber switch at the end of a cable which was attached to the engine had to be placed in Branson's mouth and if bitten would cut the power to the engine. In true Branson fashion he set off pedalling furiously and the engine burst into life, increasing the speed of the machine. Not intending to take off, Branson bit the switch but the engine continued to run. Suddenly the 'pterodactyl' was airborne and no matter how hard Branson bit the switch it would not cut the power. Branson's only option was to reach upwards and pull out all the wires he could reach. This had the effect of cutting the power but sent the machine into a downward spiral before a gust of wind caught it and turned it on its side just as it was about to hit the ground. Branson admitted afterwards that he had been terrified and, about a week later, Richard Ellis was killed when he crash-landed in the same machine. Branson, however, had survived and would go on to head Virgin Atlantic Airways, his love for flying unabated.

John Balmforth
Halesowen, May 2009

▲ *The author.*

Virgin Airways – A Brief Encounter with Chartered Flight

Richard Branson had been holidaying with his wife-to-be, Joan Templeman, in the Virgin Islands and they were due to catch a scheduled flight to Puerto Rico, but on arriving at the airport learned that their flight had been cancelled. Spotting several other stranded passengers, Branson telephoned a charter company and found that he could charter a plane to Puerto Rico for $2,000. Simple mathematics showed that if he could fill the flight it would cost only $39 for each passenger. On a borrowed blackboard, Branson wrote Virgin Airways' $39 single flight to Puerto Rico. Making his way around the airport, he quickly sold every seat on the plane. He recalls that, on landing, one of the passengers told him, "Virgin Airways isn't too bad; smarten up the service a little and you could be in business." Branson laughed as he replied, perhaps tongue in cheek, "I might just do that," but amazingly, just six years later, 22 June 1984 would see the first Virgin Atlantic flight between London's Gatwick and New York's Newark Liberty airports using a solitary leased Boeing 747-200 aircraft carrying registration number G-VIRG and the name Maiden Voyager. The path to the inaugural flight would not be easy, however, and even the choice of name for the airline would cause friction amongst its founders.

▲ *The front end of Virgin Atlantic Boeing 747-400 Jumbo jet G-VROS* English Rose *is seen in close-up as the aircraft prepares to leave Heathrow on a bright summer's day.*
Virgin Atlantic Airways

THE BIRTH OF VIRGIN ATLANTIC AIRWAYS

Randolph Fields, an American lawyer, had founded British Atlantic Airways in partnership with Alan Hellary, previously chief pilot for Laker Airways. They intended the new airline to be a direct successor to Sir Freddie Laker's failed company. The Falklands war had ended and they had identified a need for an air service between London and the Falkland Islands. Further investigation, though, found that the Port Stanley runway would be too short, so the scheme foundered. The demise of Laker Airways had, however, left an opening for a service between London Gatwick and New York John F. Kennedy (JFK) airports, and British Atlantic made an application for a licence to operate this. The application was refused following a three-day hearing after objections from the British Airports Authority (BAA) and British Caledonian (B-Cal). They now turned their attention to the possibility of obtaining a licence to operate a service

between London Gatwick and New York's Newark Liberty International Airport. The intention was to use a Douglas DC10 with 380 seats, but this would mean direct competition with Peoples Express. That airline operated a growing no-frills discount fare service and it was soon obvious that Fields and Hellary would need further investment if they were to have any chance of success.

In February 1983, when the Virgin Group was looking to expand from being virtually an entirely music-based company, Fields approached Branson as a potential investor in his new airline. The Virgin entrepreneur freely admits that the idea of operating an airline "fired his imagination", but he was acutely aware of the financial risks involved in doing so. Fields' proposal was for the airline to be "all business class", although Branson had serious doubts. In his mind were concerns about what would happen on the days when businessmen were unlikely to fly such as Christmas and Easter, etc. It would, he felt, be madness to leave an expensive aircraft sitting unused on the airport apron. Branson knew that in order to make use of the aircraft at those times it would be necessary to access the leisure market and attempt to fill the empty seats with holiday-makers. He also, quite rightly, felt the need for an escape route to protect the interests of Virgin Music, which Branson knew would have to underwrite the investment if the business didn't work out, and decided very quickly that if costs could be limited to just one year then Virgin should seriously consider investing in the project.

A number of lengthy telephone conversations with aircraft manufacturer Boeing in Seattle revealed that the company would be prepared to lease a secondhand B747-200 Jumbo jet which could be returned after one year if the plan proved to be financially unviable. Armed with this information, Branson's next hurdle was to convince colleagues Ken Berry and Simon Perry at Virgin Music. That part of the Virgin empire was well established financially and its assets would have to be used to guarantee the required investment. Over lunch both his colleagues let Branson know in no uncertain terms that they thought the idea was a non-starter. But keen to get the venture off the ground, Branson argued that the two companies could be kept separate and financing arranged so that Virgin Music's interests would be at relatively low risk and that the maximum amount Virgin could lose was £2

million. Ultimately the decision to invest in Randolph Fields' project was taken, but Branson admits his relationship with his two colleagues was seriously damaged.

By February 1984, an arrangement was made which would see Virgin and Fields having an equal partnership, with Virgin investing the extra funds whilst Fields would run the airline. The next hurdle was the actual name of the airline. If Virgin were providing the funding then Branson was adamant that he wanted his company's name included in that of the airline. After long, often testy, negotiations Fields grudgingly agreed to this and the company name was changed to Virgin Atlantic Airways. At the same time the Virgin Group's bankers would only agree to provide finance to the airline if the group held a controlling stake in it. Fields understood the logic behind this and reluctantly agreed to reduce his stake in the company to just 25%, with Virgin's stake increasing to 75%, although the deal saw him become the first chairman of the renamed airline. The fledgling airline was now at the start of a long road ahead before the first Virgin Atlantic flight would take to the skies with fare-paying passengers on board.

British Caledonian lodged an objection to Virgin Atlantic's licence application and an early meeting with the Civil Aviation Authority (CAA) saw that airline cross-examining Virgin Atlantic's chairman. Under questioning from the established and much more experienced airline's representatives, Fields had a difficult time and soon found himself out of his depth. Virgin Atlantic was still a non-operational airline, in reality still just an idea on paper, and questions concerning emergency drills, aircraft

maintenance, ability to guarantee passenger safety and financial support were being fired at Fields. In fact British Caledonian's people were running rings round him. Virgin's lawyer temporarily left the hearing and telephoned Branson to advise him to get to the hearing as soon as possible saying, "It's not going well. I think Randolph is digging a hole for himself." Branson attended and remembers that the Virgin Atlantic chairman's face showed a mixture of anger and confusion. He (Branson) felt that the CAA was looking sceptical about Fields' ability to get the new airline off the ground. When it came to the issue of Virgin Atlantic's finances, the CAA specified that a working capital of £3 million would be required. Branson's presence at this crucial point proved invaluable because he was able to demonstrate the financial viability and large profits of Virgin Music which would underwrite the working capital requirement. Satisfied, the CAA granted the licence application, but this did not mean that Virgin Atlantic would actually get an aircraft off the

ground, since if it were to fail any of the safety tests which still lay ahead, and which would be required as soon as an aircraft was leased, the Authority was empowered to revoke the newly obtained licence.

AN OPERATIONAL BASE

Richard Branson had spent several hours in telephone conversations with Boeing concerning the year-long lease of a Boeing 747-200. Having ascertained that the American manufacturer would lease Virgin Atlantic a secondhand aircraft, the airline now turned its attention to looking for suitable office accommodation and warehouse space for the engineering team under Roy Gardner to be based at Gatwick.

Virgin Atlantic was able to rent office accommodation from Air Florida at its central London base in Woodstock Street, at the same time securing a deal with Air Florida to 'piggy-back' on that company's reservations system, creating a special file to handle Virgin Atlantic flights. The close proximity of Oxford Street would make it easily accessible to potential customers. At the same time Virgin Atlantic Airways identified and leased suitable warehouse space close to Gatwick Airport. Things were falling nicely into place and recruitment of pilots, cabin crew and other staff commenced. The airline had also recognised that there was a need for someone to promote and head the American side of the operation. David Tait, who had been employed by Fields, was appointed to that role, but because Virgin Atlantic did not have an American operating licence it could not advertise the sale of its tickets in America. To overcome this, Tait came up with the novel idea of using five small aeroplanes to spray red and white smoke into the sky above Manhattan to form the words 'Wait for the English Virgin'.

RANDOLPH FIELDS – DISCORD AND THE PARTING OF THE WAYS

Despite the obvious progress being made by the business, relationships with Randolph Fields were beginning to sour. Some of the newly appointed staff were reporting difficulties in their working relationships with him, and David Tait resigned because he found Fields impossible to work with. Tait's American role included the vital component of selling tickets – the life-blood of the new airline. Tait had wanted to sell Virgin Atlantic tickets through America's travel agents. His research showed that there were approximately 30,000 of them and they would provide an ideal outlet as they already sold some 90% of airline tickets in the USA. Fields decided that it would be cheaper to use the six New York offices of the

Ticketron Agency even though the agency might not be capable of handling the number of ticket sales required for each flight. Realising that the airline would be left without a reliable reservations system, Tait came to an agreement with Electronic Data Systems, which was the then American industry standard. When Fields discovered this he contacted Tait, rebuking him for not following the chairman's instructions and shouting at him down the telephone, which culminated in Tait's resignation. At the same time the ticketing system in London, run by a manager who had been appointed by Fields, was in Branson's own words, "in total chaos".

Concerned at this treatment of staff, Branson met Tait in London – a meeting which confirmed his thoughts that he had to move Fields to one side if he was going to get the airline started – and persuaded Tait to remain. Branson admits that Fields became increasingly difficult to deal with and the two men found themselves on what Branson describes as a "war footing" culminating with, on legal advice, the locks being changed at the ticket office to keep Fields out. Ultimately, Randolph Fields sold his shares to Virgin for £1 million with a further payment due when the airline paid its first dividend. He was also granted lifetime Upper Class flying privileges for himself and immediate family, and also for his mother who had been one of the original backers of British Atlantic.

Randolph Fields died from cancer in 1997.

TEST FLIGHT DISASTER

Virgin Atlantic's board had given itself four months to get the first flight off the ground. The target month was June and this would enable the company to take advantage of the busy but lucrative summer season. However, first an aircraft was required. A complicated lease was signed with Boeing after two months of tough

▲▲ *Virgin Atlantic Airbus A340-300 G-VELD African Queen is seen at London's Heathrow Airport on 1 May 2005.*
Kevin Murphy

▲ *Pictured against grey cloudy skies is Airbus A340-600 series G-VYOU* Emmeline Heaney.
Azizul M. Islam

negotiations which, incredibly, allowed for the return of the aircraft after 12 months if the venture was unsuccessful, with Virgin Atlantic being reimbursed for at least the original cost. Indeed, such was the apparent confidence by Boeing in Virgin's ability to succeed, that the agreement specified that Virgin would also receive any increase in the aircraft's value.

The airliner itself, formerly flown by Aerolineas Argentinas, arrived on 18 June 1984, the day before it was due to undergo its Civil Aviation Authority test flight. Given the aircraft registration G-VIRG and carrying the name *Maiden Voyager* it took to the skies with all of the newly appointed cabin crew on board plus one hundred lucky staff from the Virgin empire. Richard Branson sat at the back of the Jumbo jet with the CAA official. In typical Virgin style the passengers clapped and cheered as the aircraft lifted off, and amidst the excitement Branson recalls that he felt very proud.

Then disaster! A bright flash outside the aircraft was accompanied by a loud bang and G-VIRG listed to the left, leaving a trail of black smoke from one of the engines. *Maiden Voyager* had hit a flock of birds that had been sucked into the engine, causing terminal damage. Branson says that amid a stunned silence the CAA official put his arm around his shoulder and said, "Never mind Richard, these things

happen." Indeed they do, but Virgin Atlantic now needed a replacement engine overnight to enable the Civil Aviation Authority test to be carried out the next day. Three days to the inaugural flight and still no CAA licence, and now a non-operational aeroplane.

Virgin Atlantic had signed an agreement with British Caledonian to carry out its aircraft maintenance, and when the aircraft arrived it came with a choice of engines. Virgin Atlantic's chief engineer Roy Gardner had rejected two of them on financial grounds and arranged for cheaper ones to be fitted instead, but he now recalled that B-Cal was about to return one of the engines he had declined to Heathrow Airport for it to be flown back to Boeing. A telephone call later, the engine was being made available for fitting to the Virgin Atlantic Jumbo. *Maiden Voyager* would now be ready to undergo its CAA test the next day, but at a cost to Virgin of £600,000 because insurance cover for the aircraft's engines could not be obtained without it having a CAA certificate of fitness to fly. Funding the replacement engine would require Virgin Group's £3 million overdraft facility to be exceeded by some £300,000, and even Branson's persuasive powers could only elicit a "we will give consideration to the request to increase the overdraft facility" from the group's bankers. Thankfully Virgin was able to obtain enough cash from other sources to resolve the problem, although it later led to the Virgin Group changing its bankers. Ultimately the CAA test flight passed without undue incident; Virgin Atlantic received its Civil Aviation Authority licence and now held the status of a fully operational airline. The graduation from an airline on paper to a fully operational one in just four months is an achievement which should not be underestimated, and is arguably one of Richard Branson's and Virgin's finest successes.

Nevertheless, and despite the issue of the CAA licence, Virgin Atlantic was presented with yet another obstacle to making its inaugural flight in the form of its former chairman, Randolph Fields, who now considered his £1 million buy-out to be inadequate. Fields had gone before a judge in America in an attempt to gain an injunction to prevent Virgin Atlantic taking to the skies. The legal battle went on through the night before the judge dismissed the claim. At last *Maiden Voyager* would be free to fulfil Richard Branson's dream.

VIRGIN ATLANTIC FINALLY
TAKES TO THE SKIES

By 2008, Virgin Atlantic's board was led by its President, Sir Richard Branson; Stephen Murphy, Chairman (also Chief Executive Virgin Group); and Steve Ridgway, Chief Executive (awarded the CBE for services to the Aviation Industry in the 2007 honours list). However, despite their obvious business acumen, right from the start Branson had recognised the need for airline professionals to be taken on to organise and operate Virgin Atlantic's engineering and safety needs. He was also adamant that passengers must also have a voice; a sort of 'Marketing by Trade'. It is not unusual to find the airline's most senior people talking to passengers during flights and the airline listening to workable ideas.

In a detailed interview, Steve Ridgway revealed that he had joined the airline in the early days, having met Branson when he (Ridgway) was leading the boat project in an attempt to bring the Blue Riband to Britain for the fastest sea crossing between America and Great Britain. Like Branson, he was something of an adventurer and as a qualified engineer was ably suited to lead such a mission. The two men were obvious comrades and a lasting friendship was soon formed. The first attempt at the record aboard *Virgin Atlantic Challenger* ended in disaster with the boat sinking, but a subsequent attempt saw the Blue Riband gained by *Virgin Atlantic Challenger II*, again with both men on board.

Despite Ridgway being an engineer and Branson's empire providing the airline's financial backing, both men have always stuck steadfastly to the strategy of never interfering with the engineering or safety side of the business, thus publicly asserting their belief in the professionals employed to oversee such matters.

THE INAUGURAL FLIGHT

22 June 1984 became a day of celebration for Virgin Atlantic when G-VIRG *Maiden Voyager* finally took to the airways with a scheduled passenger flight from London's Gatwick Airport

bound for New York's Newark Airport. A special guest on board was Uri Geller along with other entertainers, representatives of the press and media as well as Richard Branson with his family and friends. As might be expected at an event as important as the inaugural flight, the entrepreneur would not be able to resist the opportunity to lay on a special surprise for those on board.

As the Boeing 747-200 taxied to the runway an announcement was made inviting passengers to share the view from the flight deck of the first in-service take-off. Passengers would not be able to visit the flight deck for this, but instead could watch it on a screen at the front of the passenger cabin. The aircraft sped along the runway gaining speed for take-off, but the two pilots and flight engineer seemed to be paying no attention at all. Instead they were looking at and chatting to each other. As *Maiden Voyager's*

▲ *Vickers Viscount G-AOYP seen on the ground at Dublin's Collinstown Airport, having just arrived from Luton. These four-engined propeller aircraft may have looked dated but suited Virgin's early livery and were used on short-haul services.*
Fergal Goodman

nose lifted one of the pilots reached behind his ear and pulled out a joint, then offered it to the co-pilot. By now a silence had engulfed the aircraft and then the two pilots and flight engineer turned round to face the camera. Everyone roared with relief when the pilots turned out to be cricketers Ian Botham and Viv Richards. The flight engineer was Richard Branson himself. The whole thing had been a spoof specially filmed the day before on the airline's flight simulator. It set the tone for the rest of the flight, which Branson says turned into an eight-hour party. Virgin Atlantic Airways had arrived in style and by 2007 would employ approximately 8,900 people worldwide. The airline carried 124,711 passengers, becoming profitable in its first year of operation.

EXPANSION

From the beginning Virgin Atlantic held a strategy that it would operate as young a fleet of

aircraft as was possible; in fact by 2008, the average age of its aircraft was just six years. Nevertheless early on it did use some Vickers Viscounts and Boeing 737 series aircraft to operate services under the operational name of Virgin Express in partnership with CityJet. Eventually these were switched to Brussels Airlines, allowing Virgin Atlantic to concentrate on its preferred long-haul operations.

Business was continuing to grow and by October 1985 Virgin Atlantic had aspirations to expand its routes to include Miami and Orlando, the company successfully applying for a licence to fly services between London Gatwick and Miami. By November progress was such that two new companies were established: Virgin Atlantic Cargo and Virgin Holidays.

Virgin Atlantic Cargo initially used Aircontact as a general sales agent to handle cargo bookings, but such was the potential for revenue, the airline quickly set up its own dedicated team to take on this role. Under Alan Chambers a ten-strong team saw the new company go from strength to strength, in particular realising that the business had to be customer-led to provide a quality service and, above all, value for money. Virgin Atlantic Cargo does not have its own dedicated fleet. Instead it utilises capacity offered on its parent company's long-haul flights and by 2007 had specialised handling facilities at Gatwick, Glasgow, Heathrow and Manchester International airports, together with 59 offices in 32 countries. Its Onforwarding Network gives it the ability to forward cargo to over 100 destinations worldwide. By the end of 2007, the company was carrying 188,000 tonnes of cargo worldwide, generating in excess of £155 million in sales.

Owned by Virgin Atlantic, a new company, Virgin Holidays, was created with the idea of selling complete holidays using seats on Virgin Atlantic flights to New York and on the new Miami route. By 2007, it had become one of the largest and most successful transatlantic tour operators in the United Kingdom, in fact holding the position of market leader for tours to Florida and the Caribbean. The company also offers regular packages to Dubai, South Africa, Hong Kong and many other long-haul destinations worldwide. In 1986, Virgin Holidays arranged travel for just over 14,000 customers, but its own estimate for 2007 was that this number would rise to an astonishing 400,000 with a turnover of around £500 million. Virgin Holidays offers membership of the *Frequent Virgin Club*, which is its own loyalty programme; in September 2007 membership stood at 160,000.

In June 1986, just two years after the inaugural service headed for New York, Virgin Atlantic took delivery of a second Boeing747-200

Jumbo jet for use on the London Gatwick-Miami route. Virgin Atlantic's first aircraft *Maiden Voyager* had increased in value by some $10 million, justifying the confidence shown in the airline by Boeing when the first lease was signed, and this was an important component in the airline's ability to lease the second aircraft. The additional aircraft would now enable it to operate four such flights on a weekly basis, in addition to the successful New York services. June 1986 was proving to be a busy month as Virgin Mailing and Distribution was founded.

The year 1987 would see a major milestone reached as Virgin Atlantic celebrated the carrying of its one-millionth transatlantic passenger.

Even so, the dark clouds of what became known as the 'Dirty Tricks Campaign' were beginning to gather, and the pace of these would increase alarmingly in January 1991, ultimately leading to three difficult years of legal battles. By the summer of 1987, the two largest UK airlines, British Airways and British Caledonian, held approximately an 80% share of the transatlantic traffic between them (BA 45% and B-Cal 35%). The third UK-based transatlantic airline, Virgin Atlantic, remained a fledgling in terms of size as it still had only two aircraft. However, B-Cal was struggling financially, and in August 1987 came an announcement that that the airline had agreed terms for a takeover by British Airways. Virgin Atlantic, not unreasonably, had concerns that such an action would be in breach of the Monopolies and Mergers Commission rules. It felt that one company should not hold an 80% majority of business as well as several transatlantic routes, which would be the case if the takeover got the go-ahead. British Airways and British Caledonian made great play of the fact that both companies would continue to

operate in their own right and by September the deal received clearance for it to be completed. Branson had serious concerns that British Airways would again attempt to remove a smaller competitor as had happened to Laker Airways; this time the target would be Virgin Atlantic, which had its own ambitions to expand.

Virgin and its legal team, by now very aware of the threat an enlarged British Airways carried, found that there just might be a silver lining in the gathering clouds. What is known as 'The Bermuda Agreement' exists to govern international air traffic between the USA and the UK and includes provision for two carriers to operate services. Similarly an agreement between the Japanese and UK governments covering services between those two countries allowed for two British and two Japanese airlines to provide services. The takeover of British Caledonian effectively ruled that airline out of operating on routes that it had previously shared with British Airways. Since its parent company BA was now one of the permitted operators on most long-haul routes to and from the UK, it meant that Virgin Atlantic, as the now second UK long-haul operator, was free to apply for licences to operate on those routes.

Branson recalls that despite the worries about

the takeover, it actually proved to be "something of a turning point" for Virgin Atlantic. Subsequently Virgin Atlantic successfully applied for a CAA licence to operate a new service to Boston in September 1987, and now had ambitions to fly services to New York (JFK), Los Angeles and Tokyo. To fulfil these the airline would need to obtain two more aircraft and double the number of cabin crew it employed. The extra aircraft were both of the Boeing 747-200 series, and lease agreements were entered into by September 1988. Licences were won to operate the routes to Los Angeles and New York

▼ Virgin Atlantic B747-400 G-VTOP Virginia Plain *is caught by the camera on 19 November 2006 at Manchester's Ringway International Airport.*
Kevin Murphy

(JFK), and whilst Virgin Atlantic would have to wait another year before gaining access to Tokyo, it was able to enter the charter market with flights to Orlando, Florida.

August 1989 at last saw Virgin Atlantic commence the three services each week from Gatwick to Tokyo's Narita International Airport that it so coveted, a fourth service being added two months later. This followed the transfer of British Caledonian's four services to Virgin Atlantic since B-Cal could not continue to operate to Tokyo as it was a route served by its new owner British Airways. At the same time the

company became the first airline to provide individual televisions, known as video walkmans, to its business class passengers. A major step forward came in September 1989 when for the first time Virgin Atlantic opened its own aircraft maintenance facility that also allowed it to offer maintenance services to other airlines.

Towards the end of 1989, Virgin Atlantic continued to go from strength to strength, successfully signing contracts to lease two further Boeing 747-200 aircraft, bringing its aircraft strength up to six. The airline then stepped up its New York capacity by introducing seven weekly services to, and opening a cargo terminal at, JFK Airport. This resulted in the doubling of Virgin Atlantic's services to New York.

The arrival of the two additional Boeing 747s saw the airline commence flights to Los Angeles in May 1990 and the opening of an Upper Class lounge at Gatwick Airport. At more or less the same time, in-flight beauty therapy was introduced for passengers travelling Upper Class, and Virgin Atlantic notched up another first when it introduced onboard automatic defibrillators together with suitably trained staff to give specialised help to in-flight heart attack victims.

◀◀ Mustang Sally, *a Boeing 747-400 Jumbo jet G-VROC, is caught by the camera above Heathrow Airport on 5 August 2007.* Kevin Murphy

◀ *One of Virgin Atlantic's Boeing 747-400s, G-VAST* Ladybird, *is seen taking off from Manchester Ringway International Airport on 1 April 2007.* Kevin Murphy

◀ *G-VXLG* Ruby Tuesday *is seen high above the clouds as it makes its way to Los Angeles. The clouds below the B747-400 give the impression of a wintry scene after heavy snowfall.* Virgin Atlantic Airways

War in the Middle East

The aviation industry received grave warnings that unexpected events worldwide could have serious repercussions when in August 1990 the news broke that Iraq had invaded Kuwait, causing the price of crude oil almost to double to $36 a barrel. Aviation fuel suffered larger price increases, shooting up from 75 cents per gallon to $1.50, partly caused by stockpiling of fuel by the armed forces in preparation for a possible airborne attack on Iraq.

At the same time public confidence in flying dipped considerably; Virgin Atlantic itself had upward of 3,000 cancellations in the first week after the invasion. It was not alone, since all airlines faced the same difficulties. With fuel costs doubling and passenger numbers dropping alarmingly, many independent airlines faced ruin, but Branson knew that the big state-owned airlines were even worse hit because they were their countries' flag carriers. Whilst British Airways was not state owned, it did carry the Union flag on the tailfins of its aircraft and actually advertised itself as Britain's flag-carrier.

When the USA carried out an air attack on Libya, the then UK government, under Mrs Thatcher's leadership, had allowed the American planes to refuel in the UK. Understandably, many passengers saw this as putting British Airways and the American airlines in the front line for potential terrorist attack. However, many still had to travel and even though Virgin Atlantic's American routes had suffered a drop in custom, slowly the airline detected a switch in demand to its services from its competitors, and its Virgin Holiday package flights to Orlando and Miami had not seen any noticeable dip in sales. Far from it, because Virgin Holidays Managing Director, Ron Simms, was seeing a jump in bookings from 83,000 the previous year (1989) to in excess of 100,000 – a massive 21% increase.

Mercy missions

One consequence of the invasion was the flood of 150,000 refugees seeking a safe haven in Jordan. Through his friendship with King Hussein of Jordan and Queen Noor, Richard Branson became acutely aware of the difficulties faced by those refugees, a shortage of blankets and water being just two of the problems they faced. A telephone conversation with Jordan's queen highlighted the urgent need for 100,000 blankets (to be used for shade in the day and for warmth at night). She told him that without them, hundreds would die.

During that day Virgin Atlantic's staff managed to source over 30,000 blankets, with UNICEF in Copenhagen promising more. A national appeal on radio saw hundreds of blankets arriving at a Gatwick warehouse. In addition, David Sainsbury agreed to provide several tons of rice. Within two days all the seats had been removed from a Virgin Atlantic Boeing 747-200 and it had been loaded with 40,000 blankets, tonnes of rice and medical supplies. The Virgin Atlantic aircraft flew its mercy mission to Amman and returned with a cargo of British nationals who had wanted to leave Jordan. That mercy flight undoubtedly saved many lives, all the more satisfying because the flight had been offered by Virgin Atlantic free of charge without the airline waiting to be asked to help.

Virgin Atlantic's mercy flight to the Middle East did not end there though. Branson had come to know that a large number of British hostages were being held in Baghdad. Proposing to use King Hussein of Jordan as a mediator, he put forward an offer to fly out the hostages in exchange for medical supplies. The British government had agreed to the plan, but Iraq's former leader Saddam Hussein wanted a high-profile British politician to make the request. Edward Heath, a former prime minister, agreed to take on this role and Virgin Atlantic flew him out to Amman to make the formal offer. The offer was accepted and agreement made that the women, children and the sick would be allowed to leave. In anticipation that the offer would be accepted, Virgin Atlantic had already obtained and briefed a volunteer crew, but using one of its aircraft for the rescue flight would mean that the airline would be operationally an aircraft short. This resulted in some of Virgin's passengers having to be transferred to other airlines, although in the circumstances none complained.

Virgin Atlantic's board was understandably concerned at the prospect of one of its aircraft flying into Baghdad. They all knew that it would only take a few days of the aircraft being delayed in Iraq for the loss of income to become potentially catastrophic. The UK

ACCESS TO HEATHROW

Virgin Atlantic's licence to fly to Japan restricted it to four flights per week from Gatwick to Tokyo, with no flights on Sunday. This was bad news, as many business people prefer to travel on that day, arriving in readiness for work on Monday morning. These restrictions, coupled with rising fuel costs and the loss of public confidence in flying, were giving the airline some financial headaches and the Tokyo service was operating at a loss. The authorities had announced that they intended to allow two additional flights per week and Virgin Atlantic had spent weeks lobbying for the licence to be the carrier, but so had British Airways. Virgin Atlantic subsequently won the rights, but it would be another 12 months before the additional flights were allowed to commence.

The summer of 1991 also saw the fleet increased to eight Boeing 747-200 series aircraft, allowing more enhancements to Virgin Atlantic's services, with flights soon to commence between Heathrow and Los Angeles, New York (JFK) and Tokyo, as well as daily flights from Gatwick to Boston.

The airline also inaugurated its own onboard courier service, and became the first to offer individual televisions to all classes of passenger on wide-bodied aircraft. Continuing its policy of growth, Virgin Atlantic added to its JFK cargo terminal by opening two more, this time in Miami and Los Angeles, and more good news came from the Virgin Atlantic Cargo front. The Middle East war had seen many carriers suspend services from the Middle East.

government agreed to support Virgin Atlantic's insurers should the aircraft be lost or hijacked, but did not go as far as providing loss of income cover. It was pointed out that British Airways had indeed had a Boeing 747 wrecked in Kuwait. Nevertheless, and despite the risks, the board agreed to the rescue flight going ahead.

The chosen Virgin Atlantic B747-200, under the command of Captain Tony Ling, departed Gatwick Airport at 11:00 on 23 October 1990. On board were Richard Branson, a small number of hostage relatives, doctors, nurses, a single journalist representing all of the press, and the Virgin Atlantic cabin crew. The remaining 400 seats were unoccupied, these being required for the returning evacuees, whilst the hold contained the promised medical supplies. The approach to Baghdad Airport was somewhat unnerving since Iraq was under blackout conditions. The airliner's co-pilot, First Officer John Pugh, was taking approach instructions from the airport tower when suddenly, at 500 feet, the runway lights came on. Once the aircraft had landed, the lights were again blacked out. Iraqi officials insisted that the relatives remained on board whilst the Virgin staff were escorted along the airport apron. Richard Branson will never forget the eerie feeling of seeing soldiers brandishing machine guns and standing in line as the small party passed by, and remembers that the Virgin Atlantic Boeing 747-200 was the only aircraft at the airport, which is actually larger than London's Heathrow Airport. The party were taken to the departure lounge where they were met by Edward Heath and a large group of hostages. In fact the numbers were so high that it was impossible to take everyone, and there were some sad scenes as those remaining said goodbye. The hostages who were to leave were allowed to take their place in the aircraft and returned to Gatwick.

▲ *Proclaiming that it was 'Air - born December 2001' is Jumbo G-VWOW Cosmic Girl seen close to Heathrow on 20 October 2007. This aircraft from the B747-400 family would later be chosen to take part in a special flight successfully trialling bio-fuel.* Allan Huse

▼ *Heathrow's control tower overlooks a hectic scene as a number of different operators' aircraft prepare for their next flights. Among them are three Virgin Atlantic Airbus A340-300s, the one nearest the camera being G-VELD African Queen.* Florian Kendziela

▲▲ *On a bright sunny day*
G-VROS English Rose *is*
viewed descending from
the skies above the Sussex
countryside with flaps
and wheels in the down
position ready for landing.
Linda Chen

▲ *A340-600 G-VBLU*
Soul Sister *is seen leaving*
Heathrow on 8 October
2006.
Kevin Murphy

already operated scheduled services from Heathrow prior to 1 April 1977 it would not be permitted to commence operations from there, but would instead have to use Gatwick for all London-based operations'. The total exclusion did not apply to domestic scheduled flights since provision existed for an airline to operate such services in and out of Heathrow provided that the British Airports Authority (the operator of both airports) and the Secretary of State gave their permission. In addition, the new rules prohibited all new cargo and charter services from Heathrow with effect from 1 April 1978.

By 1991, the UK government had seen the collapse of the International Leisure Group, which included Air Europe, with the consequent loss of some 4,000 jobs. With the imminent failure of Dan Air, the government really could not risk the collapse of Virgin Atlantic, now the UK's second largest airline. A cynic might consider the fact that many whose jobs had been lost or were at risk lived in marginal Conservative constituencies, but whatever the reason, the government did abolish the London Air Traffic Distribution Rules. It did so despite heavy opposition from British Airways. Indeed BA's then chairman, Lord King, was so angered by the decision that he stopped British Airways' contributions to the Conservative Party which formed the ruling government of the day. He knew that the change could soon allow Virgin Atlantic the coveted and much-needed access to Heathrow Airport that it had always desired. His anger was further fuelled when the Civil Aviation Authority granted the two additional weekly slots for services to Tokyo to Virgin Atlantic, with authority to fly from Heathrow Airport. To accommodate this, two sets of British Airways-held, but unused, slots were transferred to Virgin Atlantic. This helped to provide a more level playing field between the two largest UK airlines, but Lord King saw it as "a confiscation of his company's property," lobbying hard that the slots were British Airways' rightful inheritance and that the transfer was illegal. The response from the Secretary of State for Transport, Malcolm Rifkind, was swift: "They're not your slots. They actually belong to the government and we issue them to you. They are not British Airways'."

Virgin Atlantic Cargo spotted the gap in the market and stepped into the breach, particularly to Tokyo, allowing the company to win many new customers and bringing in valuable income.

THE LONDON AIR TRAFFIC DISTRIBUTION RULES

With aviation fuel now at more than $1.20 a gallon, financial problems for smaller independent airlines continued to grow as a direct result of the crisis, and by February 1991, the latest airline casualty was Dan Air. Dan Air and Virgin Atlantic, like Laker Airways and British Caledonian before them, had been restricted to Gatwick for flights to and from the UK, whilst British Airways had access to London's major airport at Heathrow – a situation which Virgin Atlantic had always felt to be unfair. This was the result of a political decision which saw the London Air Traffic Distribution Rules come into effect in April 1978, but being applied retrospectively from April 1977. The rules were intended to achieve a fairer distribution of air traffic between London's two major air terminals at Heathrow and Gatwick. It was felt necessary to increase utilisation of Gatwick to help the airport make a profit. The rules stated that 'unless an airline

THE 'DIRTY TRICKS CAMPAIGN' BEGINS

Still simmering in the background was the 'Dirty Tricks Campaign' and, after the first Virgin Atlantic flight delivering aid to Jordan, British Airways' chairman, Lord King, is reputed to have telephoned William Waldegrave at the Foreign Office complaining that his own airline should have made the flight. Waldegrave's response was simply, "Virgin Atlantic offered their help." Branson considered it rather strange therefore that, after the flight to Baghdad, Lord King should again be critical, reputedly saying in a second call to Waldegrave, "Who the hell does Richard Branson think he is; part of the bloody Foreign Office?" From this point on, the 'Dirty Tricks Campaign' would gather pace.

On 29 January 1991, Thames Television broadcast a documentary covering the rivalry between British Airways and Virgin Atlantic. It described the battle for the two extra Tokyo slots and some of the maintenance issues. A subsequent BA press release accused Virgin Atlantic of abusing them, although the airline did not take any further action to substantiate its claim.

The following is an extract from a letter addressed to Richard Branson, dated 18 March 1991, from former British Airways employee, Peter Fleming, as published in Richard Branson's book *Losing My Virginity*:

"There is no doubt that BA's UK sales management had Virgin as public enemy number one. The real crisis was precipitated by the high profile Richard Branson achieved during his campaign to return hostages from the Gulf. During this period I was debriefed from a UK sales management meeting and told that a management team had been set up to undermine the 'Branson image'.

The development of actions in the European Courts has however precipitated a thorough 'cover-up' of activities. In the last few months at BA I was told on three separate occasions to destroy 'any reference to Virgin in [my] files'. Staff in sensitive areas have been briefed on 'anti-trust' laws and how to respond to a sensitive investigation involving Virgin.

▼ *Airbus A340-300 G-VHOL* Jetstreamer *is caught by the camera high above the clouds. The bright sunlight reflecting off the airliner shows how well the Virgin Atlantic livery suits these aircraft.*
Virgin Atlantic Airways

▲ *G-VGAS* Varga Girl,
a Virgin Atlantic Airbus
A340-600, is caught by
the camera at Heathrow
on 21 December 2007.
Allan Huse

Actually, the current situation is verging on
paranoia!"

The letter had been sent after Fleming had seen
the broadcast television programme.

Virgin Atlantic's own forecast for 1991 was that
the airline would make a profit of £7 million.
Consequently Branson was shocked on returning
to London from an overseas business trip to hear
startling rumours around the City that the airline
was in trouble financially and was heading for
bankruptcy. His concerns grew when reputable
journalists started telephoning with questions
about drugs being used by visitors to his London
nightclub called Heaven. When Virgin's new
press secretary, Will Whitehorn, called in to say
he had received a call from a friend who worked
at Rothschild's advising him that Lord King had
been at the bankers for lunch the day before and
was 'bad-mouthing' Virgin Atlantic, those
concerns became more worrying. In Branson's
own words, "Something just wasn't quite right."

Suggestions and rumours of financial
weaknesses can quickly bring a company down,
particularly if the suspected source is someone in
high office. If passengers lose confidence and
stop booking, any airline – no matter how big –
can be out of business in a short time; its ticket
sales are its lifeblood. Someone as highly placed
as Lord King would have access to many key
audiences, not least the national press, who
would have no compunction in printing a story
that Branson and Virgin Atlantic were in trouble.
Worse still was the risk that City bankers would
listen to the rumours and assume there was no
smoke without fire. From here it would only be
a short step before the aircraft manufacturers,
leasing companies, fuel suppliers, etc, picked up
the rumours; and all this at a time when Virgin
Atlantic was trying to raise money to expand its
fleet. Finally the Civil Aviation Authority, which
has a duty to ensure that airlines are operating
viably, would get to hear the stories.

The unfounded rumours had, by now,
convinced Virgin Atlantic that a campaign

against it was being orchestrated from within
British Airways. The airline had received reports
that members of British Airways' own staff were
telephoning Virgin passengers in an attempt to
persuade them to switch to BA flights, and
Virgin's own staff had witnessed passengers
being approached at the airports.

The 'Dirty Tricks Campaign' now swung into
full force, seemingly with the knowledge of
many senior people at British Airways, its sole
aim being to put Virgin Atlantic out of business.
British Airways repeated rumours that the Virgin
airline was about to go bust, and the angry BA
chief is alleged to have gone as far as sending
letters to the Department of Transport casting
doubt on Virgin Atlantic's financial ability to take
on the new routes. The allegations had the
potential to be particularly damaging as the Civil
Aviation Authority would not be allowed to issue
slots to any airline that was not a viable concern.
Richard Branson again recalls that throughout
January 1991, whilst the CAA considered the
award of the two extra Tokyo slots, rumours that
his airline was in trouble increased. He says
Virgin Atlantic "battled hard" defending itself
and in the last week of the month the CAA
made two announcements. First, it ordered the
transfer to Virgin Atlantic of the two Tokyo slots
and secondly, said it would be recommending to
the Department of Transport that Virgin Atlantic
be allowed to operate from Heathrow Airport.
At last, Virgin Atlantic had gained the coveted
access to Heathrow. But to have any chance of
competing against its rivals, it would need slots
to be available allowing it to operate the service
at the times customers wanted.

Virgin Atlantic now had to turn its attention
to setting up essentials such as baggage
handling, an engineering base, obtaining check-
in desks as well as coming up with an acceptable
flights timetable. Richard Branson was well
aware that this all had to be completed by April
1991 if Virgin Atlantic was to make use of the
busy summer traffic. Nothing was easy, though,
and at every corner there seemed to be a new
obstacle to overcome. Even something as basic
as check-in desks proved difficult to obtain.
Having been told none were available, Branson
found a complete line of unused desks in
Terminal 3. When he asked about them he was
told they belonged to British Airways and
although they were not being used, BA refused
to sub-let them to its smaller British rival.
Ultimately a direct appeal to the British Airports
Authority chairman, Sir John Egan, resulted in
the problem being resolved. Even so, BAA itself
would not allow Virgin Atlantic to use its own
baggage handlers. As Richard Branson says,
"A choice between British Airways or British
Midland as our baggage handler was an easy
one," and Virgin Atlantic chose British Midland.

Next an application for 64 slots which would allow it to operate flights to Los Angeles, New York and Tokyo was submitted by Virgin Atlantic to the Heathrow Slot Committee. The committee slot co-ordinator was Peter Morrisroe, at that time on secondment from British Airways but with a mandate to treat all airlines on an equal basis. Around this time Pan American (PanAm) and Trans World Airlines (TWA), who both had slots to fly into Heathrow, had collapsed. The two biggest American airlines of the time, American Airlines and United Airlines, applied for the vacant slots to be transferred to them. Virgin Atlantic felt that under the strict letter of the London Air Traffic Distribution Rules this could not be done and the slots should revert to the Heathrow Slot Committee. If that had been done, all airlines operating at Heathrow would have been able to apply for the slots.

In the event, the former PanAm and TWA slots were transferred to American Airlines and United Airlines, with Virgin Atlantic being granted 23 of the 64 slots it had applied for. However, the airline considered most of them to be unworkable because of the times at which they were available. Examples given by Branson included slots that enabled take-off but not to land or return. He told Morrisroe, "You know they don't work; they're ridiculous. Nobody in their right mind would fly out of Heathrow at 2am, to arrive in New York at 4 in the morning." Branson recalls the slot co-ordinator's response was brief and simple: "You didn't have to come to Heathrow. You could have stayed at Gatwick."

Meanwhile Virgin Atlantic's legal team had been investigating the system of slot distribution at Heathrow and came up with two interesting conclusions. The first was that the slot allocation system appeared to be a voluntary code agreed by all airlines using Heathrow. It would only take one to withdraw its co-operation to bring the system down and force the government to intervene. The second was that it was in breach of European Union competition law. Virgin Atlantic knew that if it went down the second road it could take months before a case was heard in the European Courts, by which time the airline could be out of business. The alternative would have created total chaos. Instead amicable discussions with Peter Morrisroe resulted in him being able to come up with a solution acceptable to all, which resulted in Virgin Atlantic at last getting what it described as workable slots enabling it to commence operations at Heathrow.

VIRGIN TERRITORY – CONCORDE

It was obvious to anyone who knew Richard Branson that Virgin Atlantic would find an eye-catching means of celebrating its arrival at Heathrow, and the media was not to be disappointed. A model of Concorde carrying British Airways livery was parked on the roundabout outside the airport and this became the focal point at 4am on 7 July 1991, when with the aid of a hired crane a flag carrying the Virgin Atlantic logo was lowered over Concorde's tailfin. At the same time new boards were placed over the BA advertising boards and read simply 'Virgin Territory'. Branson's reaction to Lord King's accusation that he was robbing him of air routes and revenue had been to dress as a pirate and 'hijack' the Concorde by putting the Virgin logo on its tailfin. Needless to say, the press and media were well represented at the stunt, and the subsequent photographs featured in newspapers worldwide. Later the same day Virgin Atlantic began its flights out of Heathrow, with sales on routes to Los Angeles, New York (JFK) and Tokyo shooting up by 15%.

◄ When this photograph was taken on 17 April 2006 the Airbus A340 series were the largest commercial aircraft in the skies, though this mantle is now held by their sister aircraft, the Airbus A380. Here we see Virgin Atlantic's G-VFAR Maiden Tokyo showing off its under-gear at London Heathrow.
Azizul M. Islam

MAINTENANCE PROBLEMS

▲ This busy scene at Heathrow is viewed from the Virgin Atlantic Upper Class Lounge. Three Virgin Atlantic airliners keep company with a Saudi Arabian aircraft as they await their next duties. In the centre of this photograph, taken on 15 October 2007, Boeing 747-400 G-VFAB Lady Penelope wearing her Birthday Girl repaint is seen alongside a Virgin Atlantic Airbus A340-300 series aircraft.
John Balmforth

At this time Richard Branson recalled two previous issues with BA. The first was that when Virgin Atlantic started out it had an agreement with British Caledonian that it would maintain the Virgin Atlantic fleet. As part of its takeover of B-Cal, British Airways had given an undertaking to the Department for Transport (DfT) and the Civil Aviation Authority that all existing Virgin Atlantic maintenance contracts would continue to be honoured. However, when Virgin Atlantic took on its two additional Boeing 747-200 aircraft in September 1988, British Airways quoted an average hourly charge of £61 for labour for maintenance of the new aircraft. The two older B747-200 airliners covered by the existing contract were charged at a much lower £16 per hour. British Airways was the only business at Heathrow that had hangar space for wide-bodied aircraft and seemingly assumed that Virgin Atlantic would have no alternative but to pay. If that was the case it backfired badly on the larger airline because Virgin Atlantic simply flew its aircraft to Ireland where they were serviced by Aer Lingus. The new arrangement was an inconvenience to Virgin Atlantic, but the airline was not prepared to be held over a barrel by British Airways.

The second issue also related to maintenance and dated back to the summer of 1988. British Airways engineers had failed to identify a crack

in a pylon; the link between the engine and aircraft wing. The Virgin Atlantic aircraft had to be taken out of service and a new part ordered, but the feeling of grievance was exacerbated by British Airways' refusal to loan its rival a spare B747 aircraft. To cover for the removal from service of its B747-200 Virgin Atlantic had to charter a replacement. Matters escalated still further when there was a delay in obtaining the replacement part because it was out of stock, and when it eventually arrived the hangar space was no longer available, and neither were the engineers. Richard Branson recalled that the Virgin Atlantic B747-200 was out of service for a total of 16 days and he had telephoned Sir Colin Marshall, Chief Executive of BA, to complain that the engineering service had been so bad it could have resulted in the Virgin Atlantic aircraft being brought down. He (Branson) recalls the response from the British Airways official was: "That's one of the perils of being in the aviation business. If you'd stuck to popular music you wouldn't have had this problem. No, we won't lend you a plane." The resultant costs involved in chartering another aircraft severely hit Virgin Atlantic's cash flow and, not unreasonably, the company asked British Airways for compensation. The compensation ran into millions of pounds, which BA delayed paying, resulting in Virgin Atlantic needing financial support from Virgin Music and leaving the airline no alternative other than to sue British Airways.

▲ Airbus A340-600 series G-VWIN, a very appropriate registration for Lady Luck, whilst letting the world know that she was 'Air - born February 2006', patiently waits to board passengers travelling to New York in April 2007. Jenny & Linda Balmforth

▼ Boeing 747-400 G-VBIG Tinkerbelle is seen being prepared for its next service at Heathrow on 15 October 2007. John Balmforth

1990s Recession –The Effect on Virgin Atlantic

Despite Virgin's battle with British Airways and the consequence of the Middle East war, the high cost of aviation fuel and a continued sharp reduction in air travel were beginning to have an effect on many airlines' finances. Richard Branson described the losses for the whole industry as astronomical. Virgin Atlantic was no different, and he knew that it needed a cash injection to wipe out debts totalling some £45 million if it was to survive the winter months and the threat of a price war with British Airways. Matters were made even worse as the beginnings of the early-1990s recession hit the UK. The risk to both the airline and Virgin Music as its financial guarantor was obvious. For months the Virgin Group's bankers had been suggesting that Virgin Music should be sold off in order to repay the debts now being run up by the airline. Certainly Simon Perry, who had been against using the company to support Virgin Atlantic in the first place, was in favour of selling. On the other hand, Ken Berry did not mind either way as long as he could remain involved with Virgin Music. A difficult decision lay ahead and Richard Branson had many an interrupted night's sleep.

Virgin's postcards

During the 1990s, Virgin Atlantic issued passengers travelling Upper Class with a series of complimentary postcards. These carried commissioned paintings of various locations on the front, always containing the Virgin logo, whilst on the rear the location was identified: eg 'Virgin's Tokyo' or 'Virgin's New York'. They could be used to send greetings to friends and relatives just like any holiday postcard. The airline also provided the Upper Class menu in similar form with a tear-off portion being the postcard. Today they are quite sought after by collectors. They were, without doubt, an innovative and low-cost means of advertising the airline to a wide audience. The promotion certainly highlighted the fact that Virgin Atlantic was still in business, operating to major cities around the world.

VIRGIN'S MAASTRICHT

◀ Virgin Atlantic issued a series of postcards to its long-haul passengers in the 1990s but this one was provided for passengers travelling on the short flights to Maastricht in Holland. Paul Simmons

▼ 'Virgin's Los Angeles' – one of the series of advertising postcards given to passengers travelling Upper Class in the 1990s on flights to Los Angeles. Paul Simmons

VIRGIN'S MOSCOW

▲ Virgin's Moscow – another of the 1990s series of postcards given to Virgin Atlantic passengers travelling Upper Class. Paul Simmons

◀ 'Virgin's London' – a postcard given to passengers travelling Upper Class to London in the 1990s to advertise the airline. Paul Simmons

▶ 'Virgin's Tokyo' – one of the 1990s series of postcards issued by Virgin Atlantic to passengers travelling Upper Class, this time on services to Tokyo. Paul Simmons

THE 'DIRTY TRICKS CAMPAIGN' GATHERS PACE

▲ *Airbus A340-311 G-VFLY Dragon Lady prepares to land. This aircraft was withdrawn from service by Virgin Atlantic in June 2006, but saw further service with Finnair as OH-LQA.*
Azizul M. Islam

▲▶ *Showing off its underbelly is Virgin Atlantic Airbus A340-642 G-VFOX Silver Lady at Heathrow on 5 August 2007.*
Kevin Murphy

In the meantime the 'Dirty Tricks Campaign' continued apace. The airline's financial situation precipitated a number of telephone calls from journalists to the Virgin Atlantic chairman. They had the same theme: Virgin Atlantic was in trouble and was about to make large numbers of staff redundant. Virgin's chairman regularly wrote newsletters to staff and his latest had explained the general financial difficulties facing all airlines. It went on to say that the forecast for the next 12 months had given cause for concern, but that steps were being taken to counter this. No mention of redundancies had been made and Branson strenuously reinforced this in his conversations with journalists. Virgin Atlantic had no intention of making any staff redundant. When asked how they had obtained what was a private letter, the same journalists had to admit that they had received them 'in a brown envelope'! Information was also reaching Branson that he and possibly key Virgin Atlantic people were being followed by private detectives. Chris Hutchins, a journalist on the *Today* newspaper, had telephoned Branson to advise him that a top public relations man, Brian Basham, had been hired by British Airways. Hutchins told Branson he had been approached to write an article about Virgin Atlantic's financial situation but that he felt that what BA was doing was wrong. With the knowledge of *Today*'s editor, Martin Dunn, Virgin arranged for Hutchins to record a meeting with Basham, who also gave him (Hutchins) a report concerning the investigation into Virgin Atlantic. Both the tape and report would provide invaluable evidence of the campaign against the Branson airline.

The following is an extract from the tape as reproduced in *Losing My Virginity*:

Basham: "I have a couple of concerns. First of all, I don't want to be involved in this at all. Secondly I mustn't have BA involved in this at all. I mean, all the good I might have done by saying, here is Virgin good and bad, would be entirely wiped out if it looked as though BA was running some sort of campaign against Virgin – which they're not. All right...?"
Hutchins: "It's not going to get you in trouble with Lord King, is it, if we rubbish Branson?"
Basham: "No. If you blow Branson out, it doesn't make any difference to me as long as neither BA nor I are associated with it."
Hutchins: "But it's not going to meet with their disapproval, right?"
Basham: "No, not at all. I mean, they don't care if you wipe out United Airlines – they wouldn't mind."

So, for the first time, Virgin Atlantic had real evidence that British Airways was the instigator of a campaign against the Virgin airline. In addition, more damning evidence appeared in the form of an entry in Virgin Atlantic's Upper Class visitors' book written by Marcia Borne, of Proctor & Gamble, New York. It read, 'You obviously have BA worried! I received a call from BA asking why I had booked on a Virgin flight today rather than BA. Good job! Good luck!' This proved that British Airways was somehow gaining access to Virgin Atlantic's computerised passenger records. Richard Branson received a further letter, dated 29 October 1991, from ex-British Airways employee Peter Fleming. In it Fleming repeated the allegations he had made in his earlier letter of 18 March, but added that he felt the strategy to discredit Virgin had to have originated at a very senior level within British Airways. He went on to point out that BA had applied for slots to Australia and Japan, which it did not need, with the sole purpose of preventing Virgin Atlantic getting them. Fleming wrote that BA had set up a special sales force to obtain business at Gatwick, which offered low fares in an attempt to squeeze all airlines operating at that airport. At the same time BA maintained its high-fare monopoly at Heathrow, refusing to process bookings for passengers who had flown from Japan to Gatwick with Virgin Atlantic, but who wanted to switch to British Airways for the return journey. This meant that they had to fly BA both ways. The letter also acknowledged a suspicion that British Airways was delving into Virgin Atlantic's computer reservations system. Fleming concluded, "In my opinion BA lacks integrity and this stems right from the top of the organisation with Lord King, and unfortunately permeates the whole structure."

By December 1991, journalists were again ringing Branson. This time the rumour was that Virgin Atlantic was having to pay cash up front for its fuel. This was exactly the sort of rumour that could have a devastating effect on the airline's ability to survive, especially when coupled with the financial climate in which it was operating. General practice is that an airline gets its money from generating advance ticket sales and then pays for the fuel a month after the flight, and as Branson points out, fuel represents around 20% of the airline's costs. Fortunately common sense prevailed and journalists were able to get confirmation from the fuel suppliers that there was nothing wrong with Virgin Atlantic's credit arrangements for its fuel supplies.

In the USA, Virgin Atlantic had entered into a contract with Ronnie Thomas who ran his own limousine company, to collect and drop off passengers at New York's JFK and Newark airports. At the beginning of 1992 he contacted Branson to tell him that members of British Airways staff were intercepting Virgin Atlantic passengers at the kerbside, offering incentives to fly with BA. Thomas had an angry exchange of words with the BA representatives and shortly afterwards found himself banned from the British Airways terminal at JFK Airport. The practice of intercepting passengers may not have been illegal, but Virgin Atlantic considered it to be the "most blatant attempt yet" to poach its passengers.

By March 1992, a number of newspapers, including *The Sunday Times* and the *Guardian*, had begun carrying stories exposing some of the tactics used by British Airways, but still the campaign continued. In the face of this, Virgin

Atlantic's lawyers gave consideration as to what further legal action might be possible. They concluded that an 'anti-trust' case might be possible in the USA but not in the UK, which did not have any similar legislation. In fact it transpired that in the UK neither the Monopolies Commission nor the Office of Fair Trading had any jurisdiction when it came to competition in the aviation industry, any authority they held being restricted to airline mergers. Virgin Atlantic could not even turn to the Civil Aviation Authority, since its main role was to govern issues of safety and ticket prices. Virgin had lodged a complaint with the European Courts using Article 85 of the Treaty of Rome which covers principles of fair competition, but Richard Branson knew that, in practice, the European Court was something of a toothless tiger lacking ability to enforce any instructions it might give to a company to change its business tactics. However, he also realised that the referral would at least be a useful publicity exercise.

In a final attempt to resolve matters Richard Branson had written to British Airways' non-executive directors, all high-powered businessmen in their own right, detailing Virgin Atlantic's grievances in an eight-page document. They had the same responsibilities as full board members, but also had responsibilities to act in disputes between the board and the company shareholders. Branson reasoned that court action by Virgin Atlantic would give rise to just such a situation, and that unless an apology with a promise to stop the campaign against Virgin Atlantic was forthcoming then legal action would have to follow. No such promise or apology was issued.

◄ *Virgin Atlantic Airbus A340-642 G-VSHY* Madam Butterfly, *later renamed* Claudia Nine, *is seen short of final runway 09L at Heathrow Airport on 8 September 2003.*
Sascha Kamrau

FIGHTING BACK

Thames Television broadcast a second programme covering the dispute between the UK's two major airlines entitled 'Violating Virgin' at the end of February 1992, produced by Martyn Gregory who subsequently wrote the book Dirty Tricks: *British Airways' Secret War Against Virgin Atlantic*. The programme included interviews with Peter Fleming and other former British Airways employees as well as Ronnie Thomas, the New York limousine proprietor,

▲ *Virgin Atlantic Airbus A340-300 G-VSUN* Rainbow Lady *arrives at Heathrow on 9 February 2008. This aircraft previously carried the name* Little Miss Sunshine.
Allan Huse

and, of course, Richard Branson. Despite being invited to put its side, BA refused to take part in the programme.

Hitting the 'jackpot' – bogus telephone calls

Realising that the programme might generate telephone calls, Virgin Atlantic arranged for extra staff to be on duty the next day to answer them. Many of the callers stated that they too had been approached at the airport, but Branson said, "...and then we hit the jackpot" when a telephone call was received from Yvonne Parsons in the USA. She said that she had been at home on 6 February 1992 when she received a telephone call. The caller purported to be from Virgin Atlantic's reservations department and said that her flight had been overbooked and since she hadn't been issued with a ticket would she mind changing to a British Airways flight. Ms Parsons told Virgin that she had flown to and from America four times in the previous eight months and that each time there had been an "alleged booking error". Indeed in the previous October she had received a call in which she was told that as compensation for the inconvenience she could fly at no extra cost the next day on Concorde. Ms Parsons replied that she preferred to fly Virgin Atlantic and asked to be put on standby for a Virgin flight the next day and requested a call-back to confirm she would be on the flight. Three similar calls had been received previously and she did not receive any of the requested call-backs. When Ms Parsons failed to receive the call-back she had requested on 6 October she telephoned Virgin Atlantic reservations and complained about the lack of respect and demanded to know why she had been "bounced off her flight booked for 16 October". Bemused Virgin staff could only deny making the call and confirm that she was still booked on the flight in no smoking accommodation as requested. The very angry

Ms Parsons switched her flight to American Airlines and United Airlines. In February 1992, she decided to try Virgin Atlantic again and was astounded to receive another call from the airline's reservations department because her flight was overbooked, asking if she would mind switching to British Airways. When she saw the Thames Television programme Ms Parsons realised that the telephone calls she had received from 'Virgin Atlantic reservations' might be bogus. She immediately contacted Virgin Atlantic and spoke to the airline's lawyers. The legal advisers told Branson, "We could build a court case around her alone."

The latest copy of *BA News* had carried a headline "Branson 'Dirty Tricks' Claim Unfounded". The article accused Branson of making unfounded allegations against British Airways and went on to accuse Thames Television of falling into his publicity trap. It transpired that a number of viewers had written direct to British Airways after watching 'Violating Virgin' and that in his replies Lord King had repeated his claims that Virgin's allegations were untrue. For Branson it was the last straw. He felt he had been libelled and Virgin Atlantic's lawyers agreed with him. Offering British Airways one last chance to apologise to both himself and Virgin Atlantic, Branson set a deadline of 18 March 1992 after which libel proceedings would be instituted. Once again no such apologies were forthcoming and libel proceedings against British Airways were commenced.

Possibly British Airways' Achilles' heel was its disillusioned former employees. Sadig Khalifa had worked for British Caledonian prior to its takeover by British Airways. He was transferred to BA's Special Services section and from there to the helpline team. That team was taken over by the airline's Sales and Reservations section, and staff were given what is best described as a 'behind closed doors' briefing. He said, "The team was given the specific task of obtaining as much information about Virgin Atlantic as possible. This included flight information, the number of passengers booked on flights, actual boarded passenger numbers, the split between cabin classes and actual departure time." Khalifa continued, "The team were told to get the information by accessing the British Airways booking system using Virgin Atlantic flight numbers, and information forms about each Virgin Atlantic flight had to be completed.

RESCUE –
FINANCIAL STABILITY

So secret was the operation that even the locks on the helpline room were changed." All of this was transcribed in a signed affidavit, a copy of which was sent to British Airways.

Subsequently Michael Davis, a BA non-executive director, contacted Branson and suggested that a meeting with himself and Sir Colin Marshall, BA's Chief Executive, should take place. Branson recalls the mention of some people at British Airways recognising that there was a certain amount of egg on their face. It was the first sign of cracks appearing in BA's continued stance that there was no 'Dirty Tricks Campaign'. The move was futile; by now Branson knew he would lose his beloved Virgin Music business and his airline was close to collapsing. He was in no mood to settle quietly over what he described as "a gentlemen's breakfast". Even more damning information came to light when proof emerged that private detectives had been hired to investigate Branson and Virgin Atlantic. The detectives' operations had been codenamed 'Covent Garden' and had culminated in the report, given the codename 'Project Barbara', that Chris Hutchins had previously received from Brian Basham. The court case would go ahead and was scheduled to commence in January 1993.

However, the airline continued to lose money, and with talk of a court case against British Airways, investors could not be expected to provide the £30 million or so in equity that Virgin Atlantic urgently needed. By March 1992, cash flow had become so difficult that the airline had to approach its bankers to exceed its agreed overdraft limit of £55 million simply to meet its employees' salaries. There were only two realistic solutions: sell Virgin Music and reinvest in Virgin Atlantic to create a financially strong airline, or close down the airline and make 2,500 loyal staff redundant. Within a few days the sale of Virgin Music to Thorn EMI went through for the sum of $1 billion (£560 million). From his own share Richard Branson paid off the bank debt and reinvested the balance in the airline. The future of Virgin Atlantic was now secure and the airline would go from strength to strength, ironically finding itself with more disposable cash than its rival.

VICTORY – THE 'DIRTY TRICKS CAMPAIGN' FINALLY ENDS

The legal battle over the 'Dirty Tricks Campaign' was finally resolved in December 1992, less than a month before the court case was due to begin. On 7 December, Branson's formidable

▼ *Airbus A340-300 G-VFAR* Diana *is seen with landing gear down on 11 August 2007 as it returns to Manchester from the long trip to New York.* Mark Thompson

QC, George Carman, called him with the news that British Airways had paid £485,000 into the court in an attempt to make an out-of-court settlement. Subsequent negotiations between the two sides eventually saw the case settled out of court in what was the highest uncontested libel settlement in British history, with £500,000 being awarded to Richard Branson for personal libel and £110,000 to Virgin Atlantic for corporate libel.

AGREED STATEMENT TO THE HIGH COURT – 11 JANUARY 1993

Matters were formalised on 11 January 1993 at the High Court in London's Strand. On behalf of Richard Branson and Virgin Atlantic, George Carman QC read an agreed statement in open court at the end of the British Airways libel case. It included the following:

"British Airways and Lord King now accept unreservedly that the allegations which they made against the good faith and integrity of Richard Branson and Virgin Atlantic are wholly untrue. They further accept that Richard Branson and Virgin had reasonable grounds for serious concerns about the activities of a number of British Airways employees, and of Mr Basham, and their potential effect on the business interests and reputation of Virgin Atlantic and Richard Branson.

In these circumstances, British Airways and Lord King are here now by leading counsel to apologise and to make very substantial payments to the plaintiffs by way of compensation for the damages and distress caused by their false allegations. They also seek to withdraw their counter-claim against Virgin Atlantic and Richard Branson.

In addition, British Airways and Lord King have agreed to pay Richard Branson and Virgin Atlantic's legal costs in respect of the claim and counter-claim and have undertaken not to repeat the defamatory allegations which are the substance of this action.

British Airways and Lord King are to pay Richard Branson £500,000 damages, and are to pay Virgin Atlantic £110,000 damages. In the light of the unqualified nature of the apology and the payment of a very substantial sum by way of damages, Richard Branson and Virgin Atlantic consider that their reputation is publicly vindicated by agreeing to settle the action on those terms."

The agreed statement read out by British Airways' counsel ended with:

"The investigation which British Airways carried out during the course of this litigation revealed a number of incidents involving their employees which British Airways accept were regrettable and gave Richard Branson and Virgin Atlantic reasonable grounds for concern. I should however like to emphasise that the directors of British Airways were not party to any concerted campaign against Richard Branson and Virgin Atlantic."

A statement by a Mr Milmo on behalf of Brian Basham was also made. It read:

"On behalf of Mr Basham I wish to state that he does not accept that the references to him in the agreed statement are an accurate summary of his actions on behalf of British Airways."

Afterwards Branson told the press, "I accept this award not only for Virgin but also for all the other airlines: for Laker, for Dan Air, Air Europe and British Caledonian. They went under and we survived British Airways, but only just." He rewarded the loyalty of the Virgin Atlantic staff by dividing his personal £500,000 award between them. It became known as the BA bonus, each member of staff receiving £166.

▼ *G-VROS* English Rose, *one of Virgin Atlantic's B747-400s, is seen as she awaits her next turn of duty under threatening skies in 2005.*
Kevin Murphy

▼▼ *The upper wing detail viewed from inside Airbus A340-600 G-VNAP* Sleeping Beauty *when approaching Hong Kong on 28 September 2005.*
Kevin Murphy

GROWTH

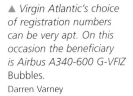

Despite the difficulties it had faced throughout the previous year, Virgin Atlantic had continued to expand its routes, commencing a daily service operating between London and Orlando.
The year had also seen the introduction of Virgin Mid Class, a forerunner of Premium Economy, Virgin becoming the first airline to offer a super economy service for full fare-paying economy passengers. It also gained another first with the introduction of child safety seats. Virgin Atlantic held aspirations for all seats in the fleet to include seat-back video screens, but realised that at the height of a recession it would be difficult to raise the $10 million to finance the project. A telephone conversation with Boeing's Chief Executive, Phil Conduit, provided the answer. Virgin Atlantic needed extra aircraft and Boeing's order book had been hit by the recession. The Virgin boss recalls asking Conduit, "If we order ten more aircraft, will you throw in seat-back video screens in Economy Class?" Amazingly the Boeing chief agreed. Next Branson turned to Airbus UK, asking a similar question about the new Airbus. Once again there was an instant acceptance. The clever business strategy had obtained a $10 million passenger benefit at no

cost to the airline.
In fact 1993 was proving to be an extremely progressive year for Virgin Atlantic as it witnessed the introduction of flights between Gatwick and Athens, the introduction of the *Snooze Zone* in Upper Class cabins and the arrival of *Virgin TaxiJet*, later renamed *Virgin Limobikes* – a motorcycle service operating as an alternative to the limousine service. December 1993 also saw Virgin Atlantic take delivery of its first new Airbus A340-311, registered G-VBUS and named *Lady in Red* by HRH Diana, Princess of Wales. Some years later, in 1998 after her tragic death, a similar aircraft, registered G-VFAR, would be named *Diana* in her honour.
Expansion was the key word in January 1994, as the airline launched a new short-haul service between London City and Dublin in partnership with CityJet using Vickers Viscounts, and less than a month later the first Boeing 747-400 seating 376 passengers (34 Upper Class, 32 Mid Class and 310 Economy Class) joined the Virgin Atlantic fleet coinciding with the introduction of a daily service between London and Hong Kong. By the end of 1994, a second B747-400 together with a fourth Airbus A340-300 had been obtained and a new service between London and San Francisco had commenced. November of 1994 also saw Mid Class upgraded and renamed Premium Economy Class.
During 1997, British Airways announced that it intended to remove the Union flag from its tailfins and replace it with "world images". Virgin Atlantic immediately responded with a tongue in cheek response by applying the Union flag to its own aircraft winglets and by changing the famous red dress worn by the 'Scarlet Lady', painted below the cockpit windows of its fleet, to include the Union flag. A tagline was also

added which read Britain's Flag Carrier, thus challenging British Airways' previously traditional role as the UK's flag carrier.

Shareholding in the airline underwent a massive change on 20 December 1999, when Virgin Atlantic signed an agreement with Singapore Airlines, which involved the sale of 49% of Virgin Atlantic shares to its new partner. This transaction was at a cost to Singapore Airlines of £600.25 million, which included a capital injection of £49 million. The deal was completed in early 2000 and saw Virgin Atlantic valued at a minimum £1.225 billion.

Under the terms of the memorandum of understanding, Virgin Atlantic retained its distinct identity and continued to develop its own products. Virgin Atlantic retained its independent management set up, but Singapore Airlines was given representation on Virgin Atlantic's Board of Directors. The partnership was ideal in that the two airlines' route networks did not overlap, but by working in tandem they were able to offer seamless travel to passengers using those routes, including through fares. Members of both airlines' frequent flyer clubs were able to exchange their travel rewards on each other's services.

Virgin Atlantic continued to grow, and on 5 August 2004, the airline announced that it had placed orders for 13 new Airbus A340-600 aircraft with options to double this number in a deal worth $5.5 billion. These aircraft were fitted with the latest Rolls-Royce Trent 500 engines, which had first featured with Virgin Atlantic in 2002 when it had become the first airline to fit them to some of its earlier A340-600s. The airline also ordered six of the Airbus A380 series aircraft, with options to double that number.

In September 2004, Virgin Atlantic formed a partnership in a new airline, Virgin Nigeria Airways Limited. This airline is Nigeria's private sector flag carrier, 51% owned by Nigerian institutional investors and 49% by Virgin Atlantic. It was formed when the Federal Government of Nigeria announced that it had selected Virgin Atlantic Airways as the strategic investor and technical partner in what it described as "a very exciting project". The new carrier set itself a mission to become a world class airline based in the heart of Africa, and steadily developed a global network that serves domestic, regional and international routes from its operational hub at the Murtala Muhammed International Airport, Lagos. The routes include services to Central and West Africa, intercontinental to Asia, the Middle East, Europe and North America.

The first flight from Heathrow to Lagos took place on 28 June 2005, and in December 2005,

▶▼ *This close-up of the front end of G-VAST* Ladybird *shows clear detail of the nose wheel and insignia, photographed whilst the Jumbo was taxying at Manchester's Ringway International Airport.*
Kevin Murphy

▼ *A340-600 series Airbus G-VBUG* Lady Bird *(Virgin Atlantic gave two aircraft the same name but with a slightly different spelling – see the previous photograph) shows off the revised Virgin Atlantic livery (the blue band around the tailfin no longer used) as it takes to the skies above Gatwick Airport on 4 August 2007.*
Linda Chen

▶▲ *One of Virgin Atlantic's modern Airbus A340-600 series aircraft arrows across blue skies on a transatlantic flight.*
Virgin Atlantic Airways

◄ This unidentified Airbus A340-600 makes a glorious sight as vapour trails form from its winglets high above the ground.
Virgin Atlantic Airways

▼ A Virgin Nigeria Airbus A340-313 (previously Virgin Atlantic's G-VSUN) is seen at Gatwick Airport on 6 June 2007.
Allan Huse

▼▼ Ex-Virgin Atlantic Airbus A340-311 G-VBUS is seen after transfer to the Virgin Nigeria fleet wearing the new operator's livery as it approaches Heathrow's runway 27L on 10 September 2006.
Allan Huse

Virgin Nigeria filed an application with the United States Department of Transportation (USDOT) to provide scheduled air services between Nigeria and the USA. After almost 2½ years of vigorously pursuing its aim, the airline was able to announce on 4 April 2008 that the USDOT had granted approval for the commencement of flights from Lagos to various destinations in America. In a similar fashion to its partner, Virgin Nigeria has continued to develop its products and now provides customers with an online booking and payment facility that allows worldwide booking.

Destinations served by Virgin Atlantic continued to increase dramatically, and 7 December 2004 saw the airline's inaugural flight between Hong Kong and Sydney, closely followed by a new service between London Heathrow and Mumbai, which commenced on 27 March 2005. In true Virgin style the airline's 21st birthday was celebrated with a commemorative flight from Heathrow to New York. Meanwhile, expansion of the airline continued with direct flights between Manchester and Barbados beginning on 13 November 2005. Virgin Atlantic continued to increase its route options, and 27 March 2006 saw the commencement of flights between London and Dubai, quickly followed by services

▶ *This onboard shot was taken en route to New York in April 2007. The aircraft concerned was Airbus A340-600 G-VGAS Varga Girl.*
Jenny & Linda Balmforth

▼ *Another Virgin Atlantic Airbus A340-600 carries the message '4 engines 4 long haul'. G-VBLU Soul Sister is seen on 8 March 2006 arriving at Los Angeles after an eight-hour flight from England.*
Kevin Murphy

▶▲ *Taken from onboard B747-400 G-VROY Pretty Woman while the aircraft was preparing for take-off at Las Vegas Airport on 6 March 2005.*
Kevin Murphy

from Gatwick to Montego Bay, Jamaica, on 3 July 2006. Further growth was achieved in 2007 when the airline inaugurated flights operating from Gatwick to Kingston, Jamaica, and Heathrow to Nairobi and Mauritius, and by the end of that year Virgin Atlantic was serving some 30 destinations worldwide and carrying around six million passengers per year.

As was proved at the beginning of the 1990s when it was involved in rescuing hostages held in the Middle East, Virgin Atlantic has a proven track record of giving assistance to worthwhile causes, amongst them backing the UK's bid – ultimately successful – for the 2012 Olympic Games. Indeed, B747-400 G-VROM *Barbarella*

carried the slogan 'Backing the bid'. In addition, the airline has supported a number of charities, and it also became the official partner to the British Special Olympics team when on 26 September 2007 it flew the entire team of athletes and coaches from London to Shanghai for the 12th Special Olympics. The Special Olympics is the world's largest year-round programme of sports training and competitions for individuals with learning disabilities, and the British team contained 159 athletes chosen from across the 19 regions of England, Scotland and Wales.

Environmental Impact

Although aviation is responsible for only 2% of worldwide carbon emissions, the industry is working hard to ensure that future new designs of aircraft will be more environmentally friendly by making use of innovative design and viable alternative fuels. Recognising that the issue is a serious and important one for the industry, Virgin Atlantic has been evaluating more efficient ways of operating the existing fleet. These include:

Starting grids – Richard Branson announced the starting grids concept in September 2006, which was aimed at reducing engine emissions when aircraft were taxying across airport aprons to the runways. Virgin Atlantic has been working with key industry stakeholders and has undertaken successful trials at Gatwick, Heathrow and San Francisco airports. The idea came originally from Virgin Atlantic's Chief Flying Officer, Captain Dave Kistruck, who had noted the lengthy delays when taxying, often up to 70 minutes at JFK and 25 minutes at Heathrow, which had serious environmental implications as well as one of cost in terms of spent fuel.

The aim is to reduce fuel burn, carbon emissions by up to 50%, and reduce noise emissions for local communities. The scheme involves aircraft being towed, with engines switched off, to a series of grids – similar to those used in Formula 1 motor racing – near the runway where aircraft would park until the airport control gave clearance for them to take off. Once advised of this, the aircraft engines would start up just ten minutes before actual take-off. The savings in cost and weight in terms of fuel carried are obvious. It is a scheme now adopted by many airlines.

Putting planes on a diet – Virgin Atlantic has been reviewing ways of removing unnecessary weight (including fuel) from its aircraft. Weight has become an important issue in the design of new onboard equipment and services. Lighter alternative materials are resulting in considerable emissions reductions over the course of a year.

Other initiatives – Where Virgin Atlantic cannot have a direct impact on reducing its emissions and environmental footprint, it is working closely with other sectors of the industry to develop models of best practice that can be adopted globally. Initiatives such as 'Continuous Descent Approach' need industry-wide co-operation, but if adopted could reduce all airlines' carbon footprints considerably. Previously descents have seen aircraft dropping in a series of steps which require repeated short engine thrust burns;

▼ *Virgin Atlantic Jumbo jet G-VLIP* Hot Lips *waits patiently in a queue for access to the runway at Gatwick on 14 May 2000.*
Paul Hogan

▼▼ *Virgin Atlantic Airbus A340-600 G-VATL* Atlantic Angel *is seen just after touchdown. The aircraft was previously named* Miss Kitty.
King Hui

▼ *G-VLIP* Hot Lips *awaits clearance from air traffic controllers at Gatwick Airport in August 2002.*
Juan Rodriguez

G-VWOW *Cosmic Girl* was chosen, was part of a major initiative by some airlines and manufacturer Boeing to try to discover a sustainable environmentally friendly aircraft fuel for the future. Also involved in the project were engine manufacturer GE Aviation and Virgin Fuels. The Virgin Atlantic Boeing 747-400 under the command of Captain Geoff Andreasen flew from Heathrow to Amsterdam, without passengers, using a bio-fuel that does not compete with food and fresh water resources. The flight was part of Virgin Atlantic's vision of what the aviation industry can achieve by using clean fuel technology to reduce carbon emissions. That vision will be further supported when the Boeing 787-9 series Dreamliners eventually become part of the fleet using engines that are 60% quieter and using 27% less fuel than today's aircraft.

Before the successful demonstration flight Virgin Atlantic's President Sir Richard Branson said, "This breakthrough will help Virgin Atlantic to fly its planes using clean fuel sooner than expected. The demonstration flight will provide crucial knowledge that we can use to dramatically reduce our carbon footprint. Virgin Group has pledged to invest all its profits from its transportation companies towards developing clean energy, and with this breakthrough we are well down the path to

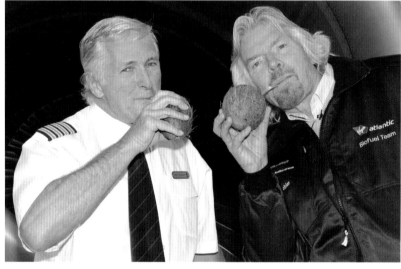

the new approach avoids these, with the aircraft descending at a constant rate.

Virgin Atlantic has also reviewed its ground-based operations with a view to being more environmentally efficient. All electricity purchased for its key office sites is now from renewable sources, and the airline intends to expand this to cover all ground operations. Additionally, it makes use of a well-established recycling programme, ensuring that waste from its engineering facilities is disposed of properly.

Ever mindful of its responsibility on environmental issues, Virgin Atlantic became the first commercial airline to use a bio-fuel, which contains a mix of coconut and babassu oil, in flight in February 2008. The demonstration flight, for which Boeing 747-400 aircraft

▲ *Boeing 747-400 Jumbo jet G-VXLG* Ruby Tuesday *is seen in close-up above the clouds en route to Los Angeles. The detail of the wing and its curve is very noticeable, as is the engine exhaust area.* Virgin Atlantic Airways

achieving our goals." It should be noted that another of the Group's companies, Virgin Trains, had also recently operated one of its Voyager fleet of trains using bio-diesel fuel. Virgin Atlantic also became the world's first airline to enable customers to buy their carbon offsets aboard the aircraft during a flight. The offset programme, launched in November 2007, is of gold standard and is also available to buy online.

In view of the airline's history with British Airways, the author questioned Steve Ridgway about the present relationship between the two airlines. Ridgway responded quickly, revealing that the relationship was good and that they often worked closely together in seeking improvements for the industry. He cited the expansion proposals for Heathrow Airport as an excellent example. Virgin Atlantic's Chief Executive added that growth and expansion at Heathrow would be a good thing for both airlines, and that even though Virgin Atlantic is much smaller than its rival it already has an annual turnover of £2 billion. Ridgway also identified a real need for more business and

leisure flights from Heathrow, pointing out that Virgin Atlantic's new airliners will also allow an expansion in the number of destinations served, including plans to fly non-stop to Seattle and Indian Ocean destinations. Finally he added that three of the UK airports served by Virgin Atlantic – Gatwick, Heathrow and Manchester – have growth available, although that would be a problem at Heathrow without the planned development at the airport.

▲ *Boeing 747-400 Jumbo jet G-TOP* Virginia Plain *is seen lifting off. The wind effect on the leading edge of the wings is seen to good effect, as is the undercarriage area.* Michael Rosa

The Virgin Atlantic Product

Staff training

To provide the world-class product to which Virgin Atlantic aspires, and which it indeed demands, it is necessary to provide staff with the best possible training available to the industry. Recognising this, Virgin Atlantic has invested in a state-of-the-art multi-million-pound staff training facility located close to the airline headquarters near Gatwick Airport on the outskirts of Crawley. The centre is extremely well equipped and provides specialist training for:

Flight crew

Cabin crew

Engineering personnel

Beauticians and therapists

Hairdressers.

The list is not exhaustive, and an extremely high standard is demanded of trainees. As with all the Virgin Group companies, each staff vacancy results in high numbers of applicants, allowing the airline to 'raise the bar' significantly in the standards of those invited to interview.

Training is usually conducted in small groups and the training centre contains a purpose-built training rig. Just like aircraft in the fleet, it carries the 'Scarlet Lady' logo on the fuselage together with a name and aircraft registration number; in this instance the name *Miss Rigorous* and G-VRIG shown as Air – born May 2007 were given after staff were asked to come up with a name. The rig's cabins are fitted as complete replicas of an operational aircraft, allowing trainees to get to grips with real-life incidents. A full-size mock-up of a typical escape slide/raft (chute) is provided and all onboard personnel receive instruction in its use, at the same time getting an inkling of how passengers would feel if they had to evacuate an aircraft. The centre also has a full-size airliner cockpit on display which, although not used by trainees, provides an interesting insight into the flight crew's domain. Fully equipped hair salons and beauty therapy classrooms are used, and students practise their skills on each other.

Practical assessments are an important part of the training and high standards must be attained before trainees can take on operational duties,

▼ *Virgin Atlantic's headquarters building at Crawley, West Sussex.*
John Balmforth

▶ Virgin Atlantic's training centre at its Crawley headquarters includes a full-size fuselage-training rig. In true Virgin Atlantic style, the rig has been given its own identification code G-VRIG.
John Balmforth

▼ The training rig at Crawley also carries the 'Scarlet Lady' emblem at the front of the fuselage and is named Miss Rigorous 'Air - born May 2007'.
John Balmforth

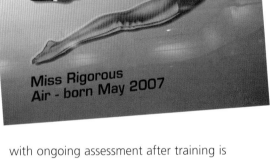

with ongoing assessment after training is completed. Any individual who fails these assessments (and this includes all operational staff, not just flight and cabin crew) has to undertake retraining and cannot return to operational duty until the appropriate standards have been regained.

In many people's eyes, the roles of Captain and First Officer are probably the most glamorous airline occupations. Virgin Atlantic does not take on trainee pilots 'straight from the streets', preferring its new pilots to already have considerable experience of flying airliners. Successful qualified applicants for pilot vacancies with Virgin Atlantic then undergo a five-week aircraft assimilation training course. The training centre has highly technical flight simulators that can be programmed to replicate most situations pilots might face in the course of their duties.

Onboard staff at all UK-based airlines are required to be trained to the same minimum standard whether the airline is a long-haul operator such as Virgin Atlantic or one of the smaller budget operators. Virgin Atlantic often exceeds these standards, its Cabin Crew Initial Training Course consisting of three parts:

Service training

Aviation medicine training

Cabin safety training.

▲ Thankfully airliners are not often involved in accidents, proving to be a very safe form of transport. Nevertheless all trainee cabin crew receive instruction to cover just that possibility. This class is undergoing such training which also provides crews with an insight into how passengers would feel in an emergency.
John Balmforth

◀ This class of trainee beauticians get some practice by using each other as guinea pigs. Beauticians, hairdressers and therapists are all given a special uniform of black tops and white skirts.
John Balmforth

▶ On display in the Virgin Atlantic training centre at Crawley is a comprehensive display of photographs showing cabin crew undergoing training for emergency lifesaving in water. The specialised skills being taught here may never be used in an entire career but it is essential that staff are able to cope with a potential evacuation of an aircraft in water.
John Balmforth, courtesy of Virgin Atlantic Airways

During the training course cabin crew undergo daily examinations followed up at the end of training by a final exam. The required standard has to be reached at each stage (the pass mark is as high as 88%) and failure to reach the appropriate level results in trainees being removed from the course.

As part of their initial six-week training course all cabin crew spend five days focused on medical training designed to help them deal with any medical eventuality that may occur on board in a calm and professional manner. It should be noted that this is not the level of first aid training normally available to members of the public and is of a much higher standard. The skills acquired include competency in the use of defibrillators which are carried on all of

◀ *A typical classroom in the engineering section at Virgin Atlantic's training centre at Crawley.*
John Balmforth, courtesy of Virgin Atlantic Airways

▼ *Trainee cabin crew seen at Virgin Atlantic's Crawley training centre, receiving instruction on how to cope with a panicking passenger during emergency evacuation.*
John Balmforth, courtesy of Virgin Atlantic Airways

▲ *In case an aircraft requires emergency evacuation, staff are taught to use inflatable chutes. Should these have to be used on water they can act as inflatable boats. All trainees have to practise evacuation whilst at the training centre.* John Balmforth

▶ Virgin Atlantic does not take trainee pilots 'straight from the streets' but instead uses this flight simulator to give aircraft familiarisation training to newly employed though already qualified pilots, as well as the refresher time required by the airline's training programme.
John Balmforth

▶ Located at the Virgin Atlantic training centre, Crawley, is this old aircraft cockpit. It is not used for training purposes but is on permanent display to give all students and visitors an idea of what life in the cockpit might be like for the pilots.
John Balmforth

▼ Lynsey Cole, a member of Virgin Atlantic's cabin crew, is pictured with the bravery award presented to her by Andy Goves of Wiltshire Fire and Rescue Service in recognition of the part she played in saving the life of a motorist who had been involved in a serious accident on a motorway.
Virgin Atlantic Airways

▲ An important component of air crew training is the ability to deal with medical emergencies. All trainees passing through the Virgin Atlantic training centre are instructed in the use of Medlink via its call centre in Arizona, USA.
John Balmforth

the company's aircraft. Onboard crews have access to the Arizona-based Medlink call centre that has 16 resident on-call doctors, all of whom are aviation medicine trained. The system provides access to more than 45 medical specialities, advice on suitable hospitals if the flight needs to be diverted, and knowledge of crew training and onboard equipment contents. A number of lives have been saved by use of this facility. The final part of the training provides instruction in flight safety, equipment locations and usage, restraint, emergency procedures and security. On successful completion of training, staff receive their coveted 'wings' that are worn on their uniforms.

The benefit of such high-quality training was demonstrated by Lynsey Cole, a member of Virgin Atlantic's cabin crew, who whilst on her way home from work was able to use her skills to help save the life of a motorist trapped

in a car that had caught fire after being involved in a road traffic accident. She received a bravery award from the Wiltshire Fire and Rescue Service at its annual awards in June 2008 in recognition of the part she played in the rescue.

The training courses are of necessity intense and Virgin Atlantic recognises the need for recreational time during training. This is achieved by providing pleasant rest areas where staff can relax in comfort during breaks from training.

PASSENGER ACCOMMODATION

Virgin Atlantic is a long-haul operator and has a three-class service – Upper Class (the airline's business class), Premium Economy and Economy – launching its Upper Class Suite in November 2003.

Upper Class
The redesigned Upper Class Suite project introduced in 2003 required an investment of £100 million by the airline. Virgin Atlantic does not use the term 'First Class' instead preferring to provide high-quality Upper Class facilities which are effectively the airline's own business class. Its advertising describes the class as a 'First Class product for a Business Class fare', although it competes with other airlines' First Class products. The facilities available to passengers travelling Upper Class feature:

The longest bed of any airline's business class product

Luxury leather armchairs which flip over into a separate bed with mattress to sleep on, so passengers do not have to compromise on the comfort of either

▲ Upper Class accommodation onboard Virgin Atlantic flight VS021 from Heathrow to Dulles Airport, Washington, is seen on Airbus A340-300 G-VSEA Plain Sailing on 15 October 2007. At the touch of a switch the seats flip to become comfortable beds. John Balmforth

Onboard bar – a private bar in an area separated from the cabin

Amenity kit containing socks, toothbrush/toothpaste, earplugs and eye mask. These items are viewed by passengers as the essentials they need on a long-haul flight. Also offered to passengers are pens, lip balm, moisturiser and stain remover if they are required

State-of-the-art in-flight entertainment system featuring 300 hours of video, TV, audio and games

Dedicated check-in and priority boarding

Complimentary drinks including pre-take-off champagne and ice creams during movies

Unique Clubhouses at selected airports featuring a health and beauty salon offering beauty treatments and hairdressing. In addition, the flagship Heathrow Clubhouse has a poolside lounge, multiscreen, observation deck, sky lounge, library, music room, playground/video games room, study, bar and brasserie/deli

▲ Upper Class cabin crew Laurence Kahan (Cabin Crew Leader), Rebecca Harman, Dominique Crispin and Amy Clarke prepare the complimentary bar shortly after take-off aboard Airbus A340-300 G-VSEA Plain Sailing on 15 October 2007 en route to Washington, USA. John Balmforth

Freedom menu offers a wide selection of light bites, main meals and snacks which can be ordered at any time during flights, allowing passengers to eat what they want, when they want

For night flights departing after 21:00 hours a special night service is available. This provides a gourmet meal in the Clubhouse prior to the flight so that travellers can enjoy uninterrupted sleep during the flight if they wish

▶ A typical seating layout of Virgin Atlantic's Upper Class suite on board a Boeing 747-400 series Jumbo jet.
Virgin Atlantic Airways

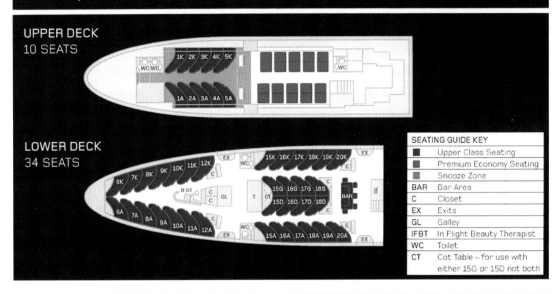

UPPER CLASS SEAT GUIDES
B747-400 (G-VBIG, G-VROC, G-VHOT, G-VWOW, G-VFAB)

UPPER DECK
10 SEATS

1K 2K 3K 4K 5K
1A 2A 3A 4A 5A

LOWER DECK
34 SEATS

SEATING GUIDE KEY	
■	Upper Class Seating
■	Premium Economy Seating
■	Snooze Zone
BAR	Bar Area
C	Closet
EX	Exits
GL	Galley
IFBT	In Flight Beauty Therapist
WC	Toilet
CT	Cot Table – for use with either 15G or 15D not both

▲ The level of comfort of the sleeping berth on Virgin Atlantic aircraft is obvious as this passenger settles down for the night with a good book.
Virgin Atlantic Airways

▲ Virgin Atlantic's Upper Class seats have pull-out dining tables and a guest seat so that two people can have meals together. This happy couple are partaking of afternoon tea.
Virgin Atlantic Airways

Arrival facilities – Virgin Revivals at Heathrow features a reception, 18 shower rooms with a valet cleaning service, bar and lounge area, business area with free phone calls, access to e-mail, Internet and fax facilities

Complimentary airport transfers to and from most airports of arrival and departure; UK options include chauffeur-driven car or Virgin Limobike and First Class travel on Gatwick Express

The new Upper Class Wing enables business passengers to speed through the terminal quicker than ever before, moving from limo to lounge in under ten minutes. Passengers now benefit from a dedicated security channel for use exclusively by Virgin Atlantic customers. After passing through this unique fast-track they emerge in the heart of the terminal building and only a short walk from the Virgin Atlantic Clubhouse. Upper Class passengers and 'Flying Club Gold' members making their own way to the airport can check in at the Upper Class check-in in Zone A of the main terminal, before taking a priority lift straight to the dedicated security channel

Drive-thru check-in at Heathrow, Gatwick and Johannesburg

Membership of the Virgin 'Flying Club'.

Premium Economy

Introduced as Mid Class in 1992 and aimed at providing an option for cost conscious business travellers who needed extra space in which to work or relax, it was renamed Premium Economy in November 1994.

Virgin Atlantic saw an increase of some 56% in the number of passengers choosing to travel Premium Economy between 2000 and 2005. In the ten months to September 2007 alone an amazing 950,000 seats were sold in this class. Recognising the need to increase the number of Premium Economy seats available, the airline carried out a rolling programme of improvements to its B747 fleet, increasing the available number of seats to 62 – almost doubling the previous 32 seats provided in this class. As part of the improvements a new design of seat was fitted in the Premium Economy cabins across the entire fleet by December 2007. A similar programme of improvements to its Airbus A340 fleet had been successfully completed earlier. Features include:

Enhanced ergonomics for increased comfort

Leather seat covers

53cm (21-inches) seat width (equivalent to other airlines' business class) – around 3 inches wider than other airlines' Premium Economy seats

97.5cm (38-inches) seat pitch

Dual position footrest

Adjustable headrest with wings

▲▲ *Cabin crew Angela Blaylock, Clare Winter and Amy Clarke find time to smile for the camera during a busy overnight flight, VS022 from Washington to Heathrow on 17 October 2007.*
John Balmforth

▲ *Photographed on the same night-time flight, VS022, cabin crew Amy Griffith, Hayley Germaine, Rebecca Jones and Rebecca Harman are pictured with Cabin Crew Leader Laurence Kahan during a short pause in their duties in the Upper Class cabin.*
John Balmforth

PREMIUM ECONOMY SEAT GUIDES
B747-400 (G-VBIG, G-VROC, G-VHOT, G-VWOW, G-VFAB)

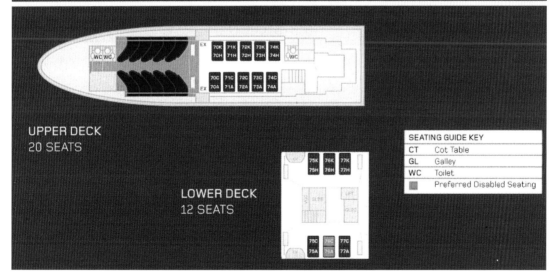

UPPER DECK
20 SEATS

LOWER DECK
12 SEATS

SEATING GUIDE KEY	
CT	Cot Table
GL	Galley
WC	Toilet
▇	Preferred Disabled Seating

▲ *The additional space provided in Premium Economy is shown to good effect in this view. The improved ambience of the cabin is conducive to passengers wishing to work.*
Virgin Atlantic Airways

◀ *A typical seating layout in Premium Economy Class on a Virgin Atlantic Boeing 747-400 airliner. The plan shows 35 Premium Economy seats, though because of the growing popularity of travel in this class a rolling programme of providing extra seats is being carried out.*
Virgin Atlantic Airways

◀ *Typical Premium Economy Class seating aboard a Virgin Atlantic Airbus A340-300 where the seats are wider than in Economy Class and give more legroom, which is much appreciated by long-haul passengers.*
John Balmforth

Lumbar airbags

16 degrees of recline (an additional 2 degrees)

Redesigned table tray

Laptop power.

The Premium Economy cabin service features:

Priority boarding

Separate cabin

Separate meal service with a choice of three entrées, including vegetarian option

Dedicated cabin crew

Dedicated toilets

Pre-departure drink

State-of-the-art in-flight entertainment system offering 300 hours of video, TV and audio channels

Wide duty free choice

Amenity kit containing essential needs:

toothbrush/toothpaste, eyeshades, pen, sleep suit, socks and ear plugs

Complimentary newspaper at gate

Express baggage reclaim

Dedicated check-in at all locations

Membership of the Virgin 'Flying Club', Virgin Atlantic's own frequent flyer club.

▶ *By far the largest number of seats is to be found in Economy Class, as shown in this typical seating plan of a Boeing 747-400 Economy cabin. Despite there being a total of 171 seats, the ambience of the cabin is still pleasant and the high number of seats does not detract from passenger comfort.*
Virgin Atlantic Airways

▼ *Passengers relaxing in the Economy Class cabin of flight VS021 on board Airbus A340-300 G-VSEA* Plain Sailing *while travelling from Heathrow to Washington on 15 October 2007. The in-seat video screens are visible.*
John Balmforth

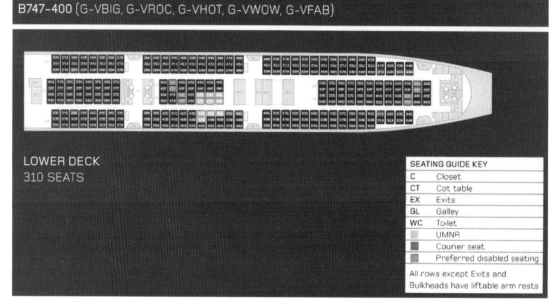

ECONOMY SEAT GUIDES
B747–400 (G-VBIG, G-VROC, G-VHOT, G-VWOW, G-VFAB)

LOWER DECK
310 SEATS

SEATING GUIDE KEY	
C	Closet
CT	Cot table
EX	Exits
GL	Galley
WC	Toilet
	UMNR
	Courier seat
	Preferred disabled seating

All rows except Exits and Bulkheads have liftable arm rests

▲ Virgin Atlantic welcomes
its young travellers.
This young lady is seen
making use of the onboard
entertainment facilities
and is happy to receive
a sweet treat from the
flight attendant.
Virgin Atlantic Airways

◄ Sir Richard Branson
is a frequent traveller
on Virgin Atlantic flights.
Whenever he travels,
he passes through the
various cabins to meet
passengers and is always
willing to have his
photograph taken
with them, as on this
occasion with the
author's daughter Linda.
Steve O'Hare

Economy Class

Economy Class is Virgin Atlantic's lowest priced
fare, which the airline says aims to give
maximum value for money. Its benefits include:

Contoured space-saving seats, maximising
legroom with an average seat pitch of 79cm
(31 inches)

Adjustable headrests and lumbar supports

Pillows and blankets

State-of-the-art in-flight entertainment
system offering 300 hours of video
on demand, TV and audio games

◄ Two travellers in
Economy Class are seen
enjoying the contents
of their complimentary
goodie bags, which
include eye masks.
Virgin Atlantic Airways

Choice of three entrées with vegetarian option and roasts on all flights departing the UK on Sundays

Complimentary drinks

Membership of the Virgin 'Flying Club'

Special features for children

Amenity kits:

Outbound – including socks, eyeshades, toothbrush/paste, all contained in an opaque rucksack

Inbound – including eyeshades, toothbrush/paste, all contained in a wash bag

Complimentary newspaper for passengers departing the UK

Online check-in except for flights from the Caribbean.

UPPER CLASS AIRPORT LOUNGES

Arrivals Lounges
Virgin Atlantic provides lounge facilities for arriving passengers at London Heathrow which include showers, Cowshed spa, business centre, lounge bar, deli and daily newspapers and magazines.

Departure Lounges
Lounges for the use of passengers travelling Upper Class are provided at all airports served by Virgin Atlantic. They are located beyond passport control, with the exception of those at Boston and New York's JFK and Newark airports, and are as follows:

London Heathrow The Virgin Clubhouse

London Gatwick The Virgin Clubhouse Gatwick

New York JFK The Virgin Clubhouse JFK

New York Newark The Virgin Clubhouse Newark

Boston Upper Class Lounge

Washington The Virgin Clubhouse Washington

Miami Club America Lounge

Orlando Delta Airlines Crown Room

San Francisco The Virgin Clubhouse San Francisco

Tokyo The Virgin Clubhouse Tokyo

▼ *Virgin Atlantic's Upper Class Lounge at Heathrow Airport.* Both: John Balmforth

Hong Kong The Virgin Clubhouse Hong Kong

Johannesburg The Virgin Clubhouse
   Johannesburg

Barbados Club Caribbean Lounge

Antigua Big Banana Lounge

Los Angeles Air New Zealand Lounge

Facilities available include complimentary drinks
bar and menu, newspapers and magazines, fax,
photocopier, computers, check-in at lounge for
passengers with hand luggage only (where
possible), TV, video and games, WiFi, toilets and
showers. The two principal Virgin Clubhouses
are located at Heathrow and Gatwick airports
and at this point it is worthwhile taking a closer
look at them.

THE VIRGIN CLUBHOUSE AT HEATHROW

The flagship Virgin Clubhouse at Heathrow
opened in March 2006. The impressive lounge,
which is more than 2,500 square metres in total,
was created at a cost of £11 million. Designed by
Virgin Atlantic with the aid of the London-based
architectural practice Softroom, its interiors are
intended to have the atmosphere and
appearance of a 'private members club'.
Eventually its aim is to give users the ultimate
pre-flight experience. A tour of its facilities
reveals the following:

The Reception Area – Guests enter via a grand
staircase and are welcomed at a concierge desk
that offers travel and secretarial support.
Concierge call buttons are available on all
telephones around the lounge if passengers
prefer to use the 'at seat' service.

Cowshed at the Clubhouse – A range of
treatments are available for both men and
women, including:

   Shave treatment – shoulder massage, power
   cleanse and invigorating scrub, wet shave,
   and tone and condition

   Facial – shoulder massage, double cleanse
   and exfoliation, hot towel infusion, and
   eyebrow tidy

   Collagen eye treatment – shoulder massage,
   double cleanse, pressure point massage
   around the eyes, and collagen eye mask

   Manicure – file tidy, cuticle clean-up, hand
   and arm massage or polish

   Pedicure – cleansing and exfoliating foot
   soak, file tidy, cuticle clean-up, refreshing leg
   massage or polish.

A range of shorter treatments include:

   Shoulder and neck massage

◀ Some of the equipment available to passengers using the spa facility in the Heathrow Upper Class Lounge.
Virgin Atlantic Airways

▲ The Virgin Atlantic Upper Class hair salon awaits customers.
Virgin Atlantic Airways

   Head massage

   Leg and foot massage

   Eyebrow tidy

   File and paint

   St Tropez spray tan.

Bumble and Bumble Hair Salon – Offers a
range of stylish cuts to men and women

Spa – Spa pool, sauna with six steam rooms and
six showers

St Tropez Tanning Booth – Fully automated
tanning or spray tan by a professional therapist

Poolside Lounge – Upper Class passengers
can relax in what Virgin describes as an 'oasis
of tranquillity'. A ceiling-to-floor Japanese
water wall runs gently into the pool,
helping passengers to unwind and relax

The Den – A games area featuring a pool table
and retro video games consoles

Multiscreen – Multiscreen is an entertainment area featuring a state-of-the-art video projection system that can simultaneously show a multitude of channels or be reconfigured as a single cinema screen

Playground – Contains a children's activity centre featuring the latest games and toys and dedicated children's television

Observation Deck – South-west facing area running along the length of the Clubhouse with large windows for clear views of the runway

Gallery – Viewing area behind the bar, which has a dedicated fumoir

Sky Lounge – Hideaway mezzanine at the top of a white staircase with loungers, daybeds and leather seating, a skylight and full-width sloping windows

The Roof Garden – Unique outside garden with great views of the runway and airport action

The Brasserie – An informal area with a continental feel where diners can choose from a menu to cater for every appetite and sit at individual tables or booths

The Deli – Offers a light new food alternative with fresh produce and daily specials; there is a 7-metre-long marble-clad table for diners

Grab and Go – Two stations offering healthy

and indulgent snacks as well as a selection of drinks and bottled water

Cocktail Bar – A 14-metre-long cocktail bar serving a selection of classic drinks and sophisticated cocktails

The Office and Library – Private room with eight business stations, fax machines, telephones, printers, photocopiers and library with antique refectory table (which has been retained from the previous Clubhouse and originally came from Sir Richard Branson's house)

Internet Access – The Clubhouse is fully enabled and there are numerous laptop points available; there are also eight Sony laptops with Internet access.

The Virgin Clubhouse at Gatwick

The Gatwick Clubhouse was opened on 22 September 1998 by Roland Rivron, Jonathan Ross and Richard Branson. Offering a modern classic environment, it is located beyond passport control in the South Terminal and is designed to offer a choice of environments in which passengers can relax, have fun and enjoy themselves whilst awaiting their flight. A tour of the facilities reveals:

The Reception – Guests are greeted and welcomed at a concierge desk offering information on Virgin Atlantic services

The Bar – Located at the far end of the Clubhouse, the bar offers a breakfast menu that includes a selection of hot and cold food plus a drinks bar

The Library – Offers a wide selection of books, with antique leather furniture to relax on. Newspapers and magazines are provided

The Games Room – A spacious room with two PlayStations, an Xbox and two Fingaboxes. A selection of children's toys and books are also provided

The Business Centre – This room has individual workstations offering telephone, fax and photocopying facilities plus access to the Internet and international financial news

Virgin Touch – Virgin Atlantic's pre-flight grooming and relaxation salon offers a wide range of facials, massages and beauty treatments for both male and female passengers, all by qualified beauty therapists. Hair cutting and styling is also provided

Cinema – A red floor-to-wall padded surround-sound cinema, which offers comfortable sofas and beanbags with a widescreen cinema where terrestrial and satellite television can be viewed

Toilets and Showers – Ultra-modern rest rooms

with showers and facilities for baby changing and customers with disabilities

Telephone Booths – Local and national calls are provided free of charge, although there is a charge for international calls

Wardrobe Area – Offers lockable lockers and clothes hanging facilities.

IN-FLIGHT ENTERTAINMENT

One of three types of state-of-the-art in-flight entertainment systems is available on all Virgin Atlantic aircraft.

V-Port – This system is onboard some B747-400s and all A340-600s. It offers video on demand, allowing passengers to watch or listen to what they want, and to start, pause or rewind their chosen movie, TV show or CD. Some of its features are:

300+ hours of video content

110+ hours of films

100+ hours of TV programmes

Showcase channel featuring the top ten CDs and a jukebox carrying 120 titles.

19 computer games, some being multi-player, including Sudoku, Who Wants to Be a Millionaire and Battlemail Kung-Fu. The special Kids' Zone includes a parental blocking facility

A selection of audio books

Laptop power points in Upper Class and Premium Economy cabins

IMap facility that allows passengers to track the progress of the aircraft, zoom in on different points of interest and destinations around the world, and send and receive SMS text messages to mobile phones and e-mail

▲ *More of the facilities available to passengers using the airline's Upper Class Lounge at Heathrow.* Virgin Atlantic Airways

◄ *The in-seat video game entertainment is as much enjoyed by adults as children. This passenger is enjoying playing a game based upon Who Wants to Be a Millionaire, the television quiz made popular by Chris Tarrant.* Virgin Atlantic Airways

addresses. Additionally there is a seat-to-seat messaging capability

Live text news facility providing passengers with round-the-clock news stories which are updated hourly

'AQA' (Any Questions Answered) providing passengers with the facility to text their questions via the handset and receive a reply back within minutes!

27 destination guide channels

In-seat telephones.

Odyssey-interactive in-flight entertainment – The Odyssey system, manufactured by Panasonic Avionics IFE, offers 20 channels of entertainment and is found on some B747-400s and A340-300 aircraft. It also features:

12 film channels

2 kids' channels (featuring a combination of films and TV programmes)

8 TV channels featuring music, sport and news, comedy and kids' programming plus the exclusive Virgin Travel guide

14 audio channels

15 games, 4 of which are multi-player

Moving Skymap display showing the aircraft's flight path

In-seat telephones (on reverse of handset)

SMS text messaging to mobile phones and email addresses.

Nova – During the summer of 2001, Virgin Atlantic took delivery of five Boeing 747-400 aircraft fitted with Thales in-flight entertainment system 'Nova'. It has 17 picture-carrying channels consisting of:

11 movie channels (including 4 kids' channels featuring a combination of films and TV programmes)

6 TV channels featuring music, sport and news, comedy and kids' programming plus the exclusive Virgin Travel guide

14 audio channels

Moving Skymap display plotting the aircraft's flight path

Bulkhead telephone.

IN-FLIGHT BEAUTY THERAPY

Qualified beauty therapist Jane Breeden approached Richard Branson in 1989 with the suggestion that 'something special' could be offered to transatlantic passengers, such as a massage. Branson immediately recognised the potential in the idea, realising that it would be an attraction for Virgin Atlantic's regular business travellers, and Jane was given the opportunity to trial her idea in February 1990 on a flight from London to New York. The trial was an instant success and Jane Breeden became the airline's first official beauty therapist, coinciding with the launch of Virgin Atlantic's service to Los Angeles in May 1990.

The complimentary service has proved to be extremely popular and by October 2007 the airline employed more than 250 in-flight beauty therapists, with one available on every flight out of Heathrow. Passengers are invited to book their treatment at the start of their flight and are asked to indicate whether they wish to be awakened if they are asleep at the booked time of treatment, to avoid disappointment. It features:

Back in the Clouds – A massage based upon the traditional Ayurvedic techniques, targeting the areas where tension is most commonly stored – the upper back, shoulders, neck and scalp. Using a series of kneading-type movements, it stretches and relaxes the muscles, and incorporates a number of acupressure points that relieve tension and anxiety and improve mental clarity. This releases toxins, improves circulation and helps to strengthen the immune system. Adapted specifically for the aircraft environment, this treatment is a combination of Swedish and pressure point massage performed over the client's clothes

Hands Zone Therapy – Invigorating massage techniques combined with the application of pressure to specific points on the hand to calm, alleviate headaches and stimulate the body's circulatory systems

Hot Hands – An anti-ageing, hydrating treatment which includes exfoliation to get rid of dead skin cells, and a mask to rejuvenate

Handsome Hands Manicure – A mini-manicure incorporating file, buff and cuticle work, using the luxurious range of Barielle products.

▼ *All passengers travelling Upper Class are entitled to make use of the complimentary onboard therapy facility. Beauty therapist Dominique Crispin provides the author's wife with a manicure.*
John Balmforth

YOUNG PERSONS' TRAVEL – CHILDREN AND INFANTS

Children and infants require special attention when it comes to comfort, safety and entertainment. Recognising the importance of this, the airline provides the following additional features for young travellers:

Special children's meals

'KiDs' brightly coloured bag containing:

watch

reading book

baseball cap

pop a point pencil

magazine

Love Heart sweets

Award winning in-flight entertainment system providing the latest selection of films and TV programmes

Baby changing facilities on all aircraft

Virgin Skycots bassinets for infants under 12 months old

Infant care chair for children aged six months to three years

Complimentary nappies, bottles and baby food in all classes of travel.

PASSENGERS WITH SPECIAL NEEDS

Code of Practice – Virgin Atlantic is pledged to comply with the 'Airline Passenger Service Commitment' – the UK Department for Transport's Code of Practice on Access to Air Travel for Disabled People and other national legislation and guidelines. Its aim is to improve accessibility to air travel for people with reduced mobility by ensuring their needs are understood and provided for, with their safety and dignity being respected. The airline has its own UK-based 'Special Assistance' department, which has responsibility for overseeing requests for using the facility.

Special Assistance – Special Assistance services available include:

Cabin crew and airport staff with specific training in assisting passengers with restricted mobility and/or impaired sight or hearing

Large print and Braille safety cards on all flights, which can be requested in advance of travel provided two days' notice is given

Assistance to and from aircraft via wheelchair or motorised buggy if available

Onboard wheelchairs on all aircraft, available for transfer through the cabin

Most special medical or religious dietary needs are catered for

The provision of 'neck loops', which allow hearing-impaired passengers to enjoy better quality sound from the in-flight entertainment system

Cabin crew qualified in sign language can be made available; the airline requires six weeks' notice to arrange this

Assistance dogs may be carried within the cabin on all Virgin Atlantic East Coast services

Two types of support seating are available for children with disabilities who are unable to sit upright. 'The Burnett Body Support' uses vacuum technology, which moulds to the body and holds the desired posture, whilst 'The Travel Chair' has head support, pommel strap and footrest. The latter is designed for children aged 3-11 years old.

ONBOARD MEDICAL EQUIPMENT

Therapeutic oxygen is available on board all flights, but the amount available varies according to route. Automatic External Defibrillators (AEDs) are carried on all Virgin Atlantic flights. The airline was the first to equip its aircraft with these in 1990. They work by reorganising the electrical impulses of the heart in many cardiac arrest victims. All cabin crew are trained in resuscitation techniques and the Flight Service Manager and two Cabin Service Supervisors on each flight are trained in the use of the AEDs. All aircraft are fitted with a 24-hour radio/satellite link to a specialist medical advice centre – Medlink (MedAire) in Phoenix, Arizona. A new telemedical service called Tempus is to

▲ Very young children require specialist facilities and Virgin Atlantic provides special 'infant cradles' that allow them to travel by air. All cabin crew are trained at Crawley in their use. John Balmforth

be added to the fleet, which is designed to be used by non-medical experts in remote situations and is ideal for onboard medical emergencies. Tempus uses satellite technology, which operates Virgin Atlantic's onboard telephone system, to transmit medical information such as pulse rate, blood pressure readings and images to medical experts at the MedAire Centre where ground-based doctors can diagnose the problem and advise on the next course of action. Its advanced technology significantly increases the airline's onboard medical provision. Cabin crew will have expert help enabling them to differentiate between serious and non-serious medical incidents and will not have to make crucial medical decisions themselves.

FLYING WITHOUT FEAR

Recognising that some people are deterred from flying because of fears and phobias, Virgin Atlantic introduced a 'Flying Without Fear' course on 4 April 1998, operated by Flying Without Fear Ltd (FWF) which the airline had set up towards the end of 1987. Richard Conway and Paul Tizzard who run the courses told the author that the early events only had as few as ten attendees, but by July 2008, numbers had risen to in excess of 170. Attendees are sat in small groups of ten supervised by an experienced member of Virgin Atlantic flight personnel.

The one-day courses are held at Gatwick, Heathrow, Birmingham, Manchester, Luton, Newcastle, Southampton, Leeds-Bradford, Bournemouth, Edinburgh and Glasgow airports.

They consist of a morning session led by an experienced Virgin Atlantic captain who talks on flight safety, take-off and landing procedures, as well as teaching people to recognise the sort of noises that aircraft routinely make in these manoeuvres. Also included is information explaining how an aircraft is able to take off and then remain in the air, culminating with an explanation of how it lands. Explanations are provided on the various parts passengers might see such as flaps and ailerons, as well as on turbulence and lightning strikes and their effects on the aircraft. Neither of these puts an aircraft in danger but can result in an uncomfortable flight.

After lunch a presentation is provided by a senior cabin crew trainer who explains in some detail the training of cabin crew. Some flight attendants are present and provide demonstrations in the use of onboard equipment. This is followed by a talk by David Landau, who has a long track record in psychoanalysis and teaches relaxation techniques. His in-depth talks about fears and phobias help people to control their worries and prepare them for flights. Afterwards, course members have the opportunity to take a 45-minute flight, usually in a specially chartered Boeing 737 that was introduced for the service in 2003. Virgin Atlantic captains and cabin crew accompany the flight to provide additional reassurance for anyone requiring it. The airline reports that approximately 98% of passengers who partake in the course are successful in controlling their fear of flying.

Following the success of the 'Flying Without

▶ 'Flying Without Fear' course founders Paul Tizzard and Richard Conway are pictured with Sir Richard Branson.
Flying Without Fear Ltd

Fear' course the FWF team has produced a book called *Flying Without Fear: 101 Fear of Flying Questions Answered*. The book answers 101 questions about flying and contains useful information from a cabin crew safety trainer, top tips from aviation experts and psychological tools to help people combat their fear of flying.

For anyone who subsequently flies with Virgin Atlantic the 'Special Assistance' team is on hand to provide aftercare, providing special requirements tailor-made to suit their needs and anxieties regarding the flight. In addition, customers can listen to a special 'Flying Without Fear' audio channel on which they will hear the familiar voice of David Landau to help relax them.

I accepted an invitation to spend a day as a guest of FWF at Gatwick in July 2008 to observe proceedings. Course attendees were noticeably nervous on arrival, but by the end of the sessions they were visibly more relaxed, helped by the organisers making it clear that "no question would be considered stupid and that they would be answered truthfully, warts and all". Almost everyone attending took up the chance to take a short flight. Those who decided they were not ready to take a flight would be contacted by FWF and offered further support opportunities to take a flight at a future date.

LOYALTY PROGRAMMES

'Flying Club' is Virgin Atlantic's frequent flyer programme which sees passengers earn 'miles' that can be exchanged for a variety of rewards when they take qualifying flights. The club has three tiers of membership:

Flying Club Red – Upon joining, passengers become a 'red member', receiving regular news updates and offers as well as other benefits. Members receive access to their 'Flying Club' account online and have the use of a dedicated helpline.

Flying Club Silver – Members receive all the benefits of 'Flying Club Red' plus additional benefits designed to make the flying experience more enjoyable. These include the use of Premium Economy check-in on every Virgin Atlantic flight, even if travelling Economy Class, as well as upgrades for the Gatwick and Heathrow Express.

Flying Club Gold – The gold tier is the pinnacle of 'Flying Club' where members receive all the benefits available to silver and red members, plus a wide range of benefits designed for Virgin Atlantic's most frequent travellers. It includes the benefit of using Upper Class check-in for all Virgin Atlantic flights, as well as the use of Virgin Clubhouses worldwide and many more exclusive entitlements.

FLYING CO

Virgin Atlantic has a sales incentive designed especially for small- and medium-sized businesses. 'Flying Co' provides incentives because miles are earned twice over. Each business traveller earns miles for their business as a member of 'Flying Co' but also earns miles for themselves as members of Virgin Atlantic's 'Flying Club'. 'Flying Co' miles can be redeemed for rewards including Virgin Atlantic flights, Virgin Atlantic flight upgrades, chauffeur-driven car transfers, London Heathrow and Gatwick Clubhouse invitations, Heathrow and Gatwick Express tickets, bmi Baby flights, Eurostar tickets and Hertz car rental.

▲ *Virgin Atlantic Captain Dave Kistruck seen with 'Flying Without Fear' course students, many of whom were experiencing flying for the first time.*
Flying Without Fear Ltd

◀ *Passengers travelling Upper Class with Virgin Atlantic are able to use the new 'drive-thru' facility to check in. This saves time queuing at check-in desks and can be completed in as little as ten minutes.*
Virgin Atlantic Airways

Airline Alliances

Recognising the real benefits to passengers in terms of seamless travel arising from the link-up with Singapore Airlines in 1999, Virgin Atlantic sought to expand on this by entering into Alliances or Codeshare Agreements with a number of other airlines. On 'Alliance' services which connected with Virgin Atlantic's own flights it became possible to 'through check' passengers and baggage to their final destination, provided local customs and regulations permitted it. Although travellers still had to change aircraft, it was no longer necessary to reclaim baggage and check in again at interchange airports – a major benefit for passengers. Virgin Atlantic synchronised its own schedules with those of the 'Alliance' partners, enabling the shortest possible connections to be made. Finally, in similar manner to the partnership with Singapore Airlines, passengers became able to earn and redeem 'Flying Club' miles on 'Alliance' services, subject to individual agreements.

Agreements were in place with the following airlines by the end of 2007:

Singapore Airlines
The agreement with Singapore Airlines enabled Virgin Atlantic passengers to purchase tickets in Economy and Business Classes on Singapore Airlines services from both Heathrow and Manchester to Singapore. Similarly Singapore Airlines passengers are able to purchase seats on Virgin Atlantic transatlantic flights between Singapore and Orlando, Boston, Miami and Washington as well as London to Los Angeles, San Francisco or Dubai. In January 2007, it became possible for Virgin Atlantic passengers to travel on Singapore Airlines services between London and Sydney, Australia.

bmi British Midland
The arrangement with bmi British Midland allows European passengers greater access and simple connections into Virgin Atlantic services from Heathrow. In return the airline is able to offer connections from its own services into Amsterdam, Brussels, Dublin, Hanover, Palma, Paris and Venice, although the list is not exhaustive.

Continental Airlines
Virgin Atlantic's Codeshare Agreement with Continental Airlines allows the two to offer, jointly, high-quality higher frequency services to New York. Virgin Atlantic is able to sell seats in Economy and Business First on two of Continental Airlines' services from Gatwick to Newark, providing a total of seven daily services to New York. In addition, Virgin passengers can now book through to ten American domestic destinations.

South African Airways
Under this agreement, passengers using Virgin Atlantic services to and from Johannesburg can connect into South African Airways services between Johannesburg and Cape Town, Durban, Port Elizabeth and East London.

America West Airlines/US Airways
Virgin Atlantic's Codeshare Agreement with America West Airlines/US Airways provides its passengers with convenient connections with services to and from Phoenix and San Diego into Virgin Atlantic services to and from Los Angeles, San Francisco and Las Vegas.

Virgin Blue
Despite its name, Virgin Blue has no direct relationship with Virgin Atlantic, although Virgin Atlantic's parent company, the Virgin Group, does hold a stake, enabling the Virgin brand name to be used. The Alliance Agreement with Virgin Blue is valuable as it allows passengers to connect with services to and from Sydney and Hong Kong into Virgin Blue flights to and from Brisbane, Adelaide, Cairns, Melbourne and Gold Coast domestic flights.

Air China
The Codeshare Agreement with Air China enables Virgin Atlantic passengers to purchase flights between Heathrow and Beijing, which complement its own flights to Shanghai. Conversely Air China passengers can obtain flights on Virgin Atlantic's route between Heathrow and Shanghai.

Air Jamaica
A new alliance introduced in November 2007 followed the introduction of Virgin Atlantic flights between Gatwick and Kingston a month earlier. Air Jamaica placed its code on Virgin Atlantic flights operating to and from Kingston and Montego Bay as well as on

internal flights between Montego Bay and Kingston. This resulted in travellers being able to choose from four direct services each week to the island, more than any other carrier, as well as taking advantage of flights between Jamaica's two key cities. The Codeshare also applied to Virgin Atlantic's flights between Miami and London Heathrow, and includes links between the two carriers' frequent flyer clubs, '7th Heaven' and 'Flying Club'. At the time of signing, Steve Ridgway, Virgin Atlantic's Chief Executive, commented that Virgin Atlantic already had "a big

commitment to the Caribbean and a strong relationship with the local people allowing the tourist industry to benefit significantly from the agreement".

All Nippon Airways
Virgin Atlantic's Alliance Agreement with All Nippon Airways (ANA) allows Virgin Atlantic passengers to fly onwards in Japan on ANA's domestic services. The deal also allows for Air Nippon Airways travellers to fly on Virgin Atlantic services from All Nippon Airways destinations elsewhere on the Virgin route network.

▲ *G-VHOL Jetstreamer's tailfin detail is shown with great clarity. Also visible is the marker light on the wing tip and the lettering 'OL' at the top of the fin which are the last two letters of the aircraft registration number.*
Virgin Atlantic Airways

THE VIRGIN ATLANTIC FLEET

The average age of the fleet in July 2008 was just 6 years and 10 months, and it consisted of 38 aircraft: six Airbus A340-300s, 19 Airbus A340-600s and 13 Boeing 747-400s.

BOEING 747-400 SERIES

▶ *The sheer size of Boeing 747-400 aircraft is obvious in this view of G-VROS* English Rose *taken at Manchester Ringway International Airport on 8 July 2007. The undercarriage is shown in great detail as the aircraft begins to turn right to its berthing point. The height above ground of the pilots' cockpit and angles of the tailplane are also evident.*
Kevin Murphy

▼ *Jumbo jet G-VGAL* Jersey Girl *is seen departing from Manchester Ringway International Airport into a miserable-looking sky on 28 May 2005, carrying the message on her fuselage side* 'Fly a younger fleet'.
Kevin Murphy

▼▶ *The massive size of a Boeing 747-400 aircraft is again illustrated here as G-VLIP* Hot Lips *takes off at Manchester on 16 January 2006.*
Kevin Murphy

All Virgin Atlantic services out of Gatwick and Manchester airports are operated by Boeing 747-400 aircraft, the Airbus models being operated from Heathrow. The aircraft, nicknamed 'Jumbo jet', is one of the most easily recognised in the world and was the first wide-bodied commercial airliner to be produced. Built by Boeing's Commercial Airplane Unit in Seattle, USA, its first commercial flight (B747-100) was in 1970, although its development had begun in 1963 when the US Military was looking for a larger strategic transport aircraft, and it held the passenger capacity record for some 37 years until Airbus launched its A380.

In the 1960s, air travel was witnessing impressive growth, and seeing the need to design a newer, larger and faster aircraft for

long-haul flight, Boeing transferred its B737 development team manager, Joe Sutter, to manage development of a new airliner – the Boeing 747. This was taking place against the background of new designs of supersonic aircraft, which it was assumed would take over passenger-carrying duties from the B747 and resulted in the freight version of the Jumbo arriving on the scene. This protected Boeing's ability to maintain a production line if sales of the passenger version dropped. In fact the B747 continued to be the commercial passenger choice for many airlines. Natural development saw a number of derivatives, including the B747-200 series used by Virgin Atlantic in its earlier days, although in today's fleet the Jumbos are all of the B747-400 series. By March 2008, some 1,400 of the type had been built, reinforcing the view that the B747-400 was popular with operators and passengers alike.

The airliner is double-decked for part of its length, the upper deck creating the clearly defined 'hump' at the front of the fuselage. Whilst this allows for extra seating, it also provides a front cargo door on the freight versions. This was important because designers had concerns that in the event of a crash-landing there was a real risk that cargo could move forward and crush the pilots if they were located in a cockpit in the conventional position. When it entered service the B747-400 was amongst the fastest airliners around, having a sub-sonic cruising speed of 0.85 Mach (567 mph/913 km/h). The B747-400 aircraft used by Virgin Atlantic are powered by four GE CF6-80C engines. Despite carrying more than 57,000 gallons of fuel, the B747-400 series consumes up to 13% less fuel than previous versions,

and engine noise levels are half that of the original B747s built in the 1970s. Typical maximum range is 7,000nm with a full payload of passengers.

The sheer size of the aircraft did give rise to some concerns about its flyability, and to address these a high level of structural redundancy was included in the design which provided four redundant hydraulic systems. It was also given quadruple main landing gear with 16 wheels and dual-control surfaces as well as the most advanced high-lift devices available to allow it to operate from existing airports. These included leading edge slats running almost the entire length of the wing plus complex slotted flaps along the rear.

The B747 development caused a few headaches for Boeing because it simply did not have a plant large enough in which to assemble the giant airliner. The solution was to build a new plant some 30 miles north of Seattle on a 780-acre site in June 1966, with some 4 million cubic yards of earth moved in the site-levelling process. By September 1968, the world's press witnessed the first B747 rolled out in front of the representatives of 26 interested airlines and by December 1969, the airliner had received the much-needed certificate of airworthiness from the Federal Aviation Administration (FAA). The overall development costs had been huge and

Boeing had to borrow heavily, with repeated requests for further funding during the final months leading up to delivery of the first aircraft to Pan American which entered service on that airline's New York to London route on 22 January 1970. Had the funding requests been refused, the whole financial viability of Boeing would have come into question. However, the project provided a hugely successful aircraft which gave Boeing a monopoly in large aircraft production for several years. The gamble had paid off.

By 1985, development of the longer-range B747-400, which features so strongly in the Virgin Atlantic fleet, had commenced, having a revamped cockpit which required a crew of two instead of three in the previous versions. Amazingly the number of dials, gauges and switches in the cockpit was reduced from 971 to just 365. The new design was a large wide-bodied airliner with four engines mounted on the wings which have a high sweep angle of 37.5 degrees, giving a fast efficient cruise at Mach 0.84 and wing tip extensions of 6 feet (1.8m) and winglets of the same size. The wing sweep also meant that the B747-400 would be able to use existing hangars. The passenger version entered service in February 1989, featuring in the Virgin Atlantic fleet just five years later with the brand new arrivals of G-VFAB *Lady Penelope* and G-VHOT *Tubular Belle*.

▲ *Although not yet delivered, this is a manufactured image of what the Boeing 787-900 Dreamliners will look like in Virgin Atlantic service.*
Virgin Atlantic Airways

▲ *Creative use of photographic media creates another view of how a B787-900 Dreamliner will appear in service.*
Virgin Atlantic Airways

BOEING 787-9 DREAMLINERS

Conscious of the need to maintain one of the world's youngest fleets, Virgin Atlantic announced on 24 April 2007 that it had placed an order for 15 new Boeing 787-9 series Dreamliners with an option for a further eight and purchase rights on another 20 in a deal worth up to $8 billion. Virgin Atlantic's Dreamliner order was the first by a UK airline and the largest by any European competitor. The new airliner will be configured to Virgin Atlantic's three-class requirement and will be able to carry up to 290 passengers.

Four key technologies contribute to fuel efficiency, resulting in the new Dreamliners ordered by Virgin Atlantic burning some 27% less fuel per passenger than the Airbus A340-300 series which they will replace:

New engines

Increased use of lighter materials

More efficient systems applications

Highly advanced aerodynamics.

More than half of the aircraft is constructed from composite materials, resulting in significant weight reduction and a consequent reduction in fuel used and carbon emissions. Its noise footprint is known to be 60% lower than the Airbus A340-300, benefiting communities living near airports from which it will operate. This is aided by acoustically treated engine inlets and chevrons along with distinctive serrated edges at the back of the engine cowling, which are designed to keep sound within airport boundaries.

The aircraft's engines will be manufactured by either General Electric or Rolls-Royce. The 787-9 series aircraft will be able to travel 8,500nm without refuelling.

Not only will the new additions to the fleet enable replacement of older aircraft, they will also assist the airline's plans for growth with its aspirations to operate services to destinations like Rio de Janeiro, Seattle, Vancouver, Bangkok and Melbourne. The long-range capacity of the B787-9 series also gives potential for non-stop flights from London to Perth in Western Australia and Honolulu in Hawaii, making them economical for the first time in the airline's history. The aircraft made its world debut on 8 July 2007 and on the same day Virgin Atlantic converted its eight purchase options into firm orders, making a total of 23 in all. They are expected to operate from all three of Virgin Atlantic's UK bases at Heathrow, Gatwick and Manchester airports.

The B787-9 will provide passengers with the following:

- More space – wider aisles and higher ceilings
- The largest windows in the air, offering passengers seated throughout the aircraft impressive views
- Larger overhead storage, better lighting and more headroom
- Lower cabin altitude and a smoother ride
- New technologies to improve air purification and humidity
- Improvements in level and quality of noise, making the aircraft quieter for passengers and crew.

Airbus A340-300

The Airbus A340 family of wide-bodied four-engined aircraft is optimised for long-range performance and is in service with many airlines, including Virgin Atlantic, for use on non-stop long-haul services.

The A340 was the longest-range aircraft in the world until 2007, and the first aircraft to be built by Airbus with four engines. First introduced in 1993, the aircraft was added to the Branson fleet in the same year, Virgin Atlantic being the first UK airline to do so.

It operates six A340-300 series aircraft which each carry 255 passengers up to a distance of 7,500nm. The fuselage is based on the A300 and A310 aircraft: wide enough for passenger comfort but slim enough for optimum fuel efficiency. The A340 also has the most slender wings of any aircraft and large fuel-saving winglets. BAE Systems, which has a 20% share in Airbus, is responsible for the aerodynamic design and manufacture of the wing for all of the company's aircraft. The Airbus A340-300 series is powered by four CFM International CFM56-5C2 or 5C4 engines delivering either 31,200lb or 34,000lb of thrust respectively.

The flight deck incorporates an optimised layout of liquid crystal displays making it easier for flight crew to assimilate all relevant data. Its 6.25 sq inch screens have made eye-scanning a thing of the past. The new Electronic Flight Instrument System (EFIS) provides flight information and consists of Primary Flight Display and a Navigation Display for each pilot. Included are three multi-purpose control and display units giving access to the aircraft's flight management system. These can provide maintenance data both in the air and on the ground. An Electronic Centralised Aircraft Monitor (ECAM) provides an engine warning display on the upper screen and the aircraft systems display on the lower screen. Essential data is rearranged by an automatic

▼ *A superb photograph of Virgin Atlantic's Airbus A340-300 airliner G-VHOL Jetstreamer, showing the aircraft flying above the clouds. From this angle the 'cigar-like' tube of the fuselage is accentuated.*
Virgin Atlantic Airways

▲▲ Airbus A340-600 series G-VGOA Indian Princess is pictured against threatening skies above Heathrow Airport on 3 July 2007.
Allan Huse

▲ Superbly named Airbus A340-600 G-VEIL Queen of the Skies is seen with landing gear down at Heathrow on 7 August 2004. The message on the rear of the fuselage reads '4 engines 4 long haul'.
Allan Huse

display reconfiguration in the event of a display unit failure, and the flight deck is also fitted with an integrated standby instrumentation system. The flight deck incorporates a multi-purpose printer, a Ground Proximity Warning System (GPWS), an Aircraft Communications Addressing and Reporting System (ACARS), a Global Positioning System (GPS), satellite communications, Traffic Collision Avoidance System (TCAS), a Forward Air Navigator System (FANS A) and an optional Microwave Landing System (MLS).

The airliner's flight control system provides substantial operational benefits including reduced pilot workload, enhanced overall performance through reduced pilot control inputs, improved smoothness and stability as well as better fuel economy through the optimised deflection of control surfaces and reduced drag. The system incorporates multiple redundancy

and a high degree of integrity. There are three primary and two secondary main computers, each comprising two units with different software. The primary and secondary computers have different hardware and different architectures. The power supply sources and the signalling lanes are segregated. Mechanical signalling is retained for rudder movement and for the horizontal stabiliser trim, and the aircraft can, if necessary, be flown on mechanical systems only.

The A340 fuselage structure is mainly of high-strength aluminium alloy, but with some structures of carbon fibre and glass fibre-reinforced plastics. The use of advanced composite materials for components including the fin and rudder, horizontal tailplane, wing trailing edge moving surfaces, the wing/fuselage fairing and the cabin floor panels results in reduced weight and fuel burn.

AIRBUS A340-600

The commercial launch for the A340-600 was at the 1997 Paris Air Show, the same year that Virgin Atlantic became the worldwide launch airline by ordering eight of the aircraft with an option for eight more. Intended to be an early-generation replacement for the Boeing 747, the A340-600 has similar capacity but twice the cargo volume and lower trip and seat costs. With its first commercial passenger flight being on 23 April 2001, the first of the newly designed A340-600 series ordered by Richard Branson's airline was delivered to Virgin Atlantic at the

▲▲ Virgin Atlantic Captain Barry
Wong is seen at the controls
of G-VSEA Plain Sailing as he
prepares to command flight
VS021 en route to Washington on
15 October 2007. The complexity
of the controls to the layman
is obvious. John Balmforth

◄ More of the controls of the
Airbus A340-300 aircraft which
Captain Wong and his co-pilot will
need to use during the flight.
John Balmforth

▲ The co-pilot on flight VS021
was First Officer Ian Reid. It can
be seen that the control panel
screens in front of the Captain
are repeated on the panel
in front of the First Officer,
necessary when he takes his
turn at the controls during
a long-haul flight.
John Balmforth

▲ A wonderful view of
Airbus A340-642 G-VOGE
Cover Girl seen
approaching Heathrow's
runway 27L on
12 August 2007.
Paul Massey

▶ A340-600 G-VWKD
Miss Behavin is caught
taking time out to
sunbathe near the beach
whilst the fuselage
proclaims '4 engines 4
long haul' at Sydney's
Kingsford International
Airport, Australia.
Mark Thompson

2002 Farnborough International Air Show, entering service shortly afterwards in July 2002. It retains the same fuselage cross-section as its A340-300 series predecessor but is some 11.6 metres longer, at 75.3 metres, making it the longest civil aircraft produced and over 4 metres longer than the B747 Jumbo jet. The A340-600 series is fitted with a modified wing, increasing its wingspan to 63.4 metres. It makes use of many of the earlier A340 versions' innovations, including the high degree of redundancy built into its computer control systems, but additionally has a 'fly-by-wire' control facility fitted, making the aircraft easier for pilots to fly. The ultra-long A340-600 was the first aircraft to

see the use of composite materials on crucial primary structures such as the rear pressure bulkhead and the keel beam. Composites are also to be found in the fin and rudder, horizontal tailplane and wing trailing edge surfaces as well as the floor panels in the passenger deck.

The new Airbus is designed to fly up to 7,250nm with a full payload of passengers, the Virgin Atlantic model being configured with 308 seats in its three-class layout. Power is supplied by four Rolls-Royce Trent 500 engines each delivering 56,000lb of thrust. The aircraft also benefits from some of the latest manufacturing techniques such as laser beam welding. The A340-600 has an additional four-wheel

▲ *Seen just completing the stowing of its landing gear after take-off from Heathrow Airport on 5 August 2007 is Airbus A340-600 G-VWEB Surfer Girl.* Kevin Murphy

undercarriage unit located on the fuselage centre line to cope with the increase in Maximum Take-Off Weight (MTOW). The first seven A340-600 aircraft delivered to Virgin Atlantic were found to have overweight wings and the airline elected to receive replacement aircraft, the originals being delivered at reduced cost to Iberia Airlines and Cathay Pacific.

AIRBUS A380-800 'SUPER JUMBO'

Virgin Atlantic Airways had also ordered six of the Airbus A380 series aircraft, with options to double that number. Initially delivery had been anticipated for October 2006, but the projected date was delayed to 2009. Steve Ridgway told the author that whilst the A380s are still on order, Virgin Atlantic has deferred this to 2012/13 with the agreement of Airbus. He said, "It suits both parties well because it will allow the builder to concentrate on its existing large order book from Singapore Airlines and the like, whilst at the same time allowing Virgin Atlantic to

evaluate the aircraft as it enters service." Virgin Atlantic intends to use these new aircraft on the routes from London to Hong Kong, Los Angeles, New York, San Francisco, Sydney and Tokyo. For the immediate future the leases on the Boeing 747-400s will be extended. Ridgway revealed that when fitted out to the Virgin Atlantic design, the aircraft would seat between 480 and 520 passengers. Virgin Atlantic is also considering the possibility of including casinos, double beds and gymnasiums on its version of the aircraft.

The A380 is the largest commercial airliner in the world and will eventually appear in two versions. The A380-800 series is a passenger airliner, whilst the A380-800F series will be for freight. The aircraft is quite innovative, using aluminium power cables instead of copper, and features bulbless illumination, using LEDs in the cabin, cockpit, cargo and other fuselage areas. Some 75% of the fuselage is made of

◄ *An overhead view of Virgin Atlantic Airbus A340-642 G-VOGE Cover Girl standing on the concrete at Heathrow Airport on 18 May 2007.* Chris Lofting

'Airport Compatibility' and full compatibility was always a key driver in the A380's development. From the early design phase in 1996, Airbus established an ongoing dialogue with regulators, airports, airlines, ground handlers and trade associations. That the overall objective to make it compliant with the environs of the average airport has been achieved is a success in itself, and means that the A380 can be integrated with ease into existing airport facilities. The airliner makes full use of its larger wingspan and wing area, which gives greater lift during take-off, and is powered by either the Engine Alliance GP7270 or Trent 970B/972B engines. As a consequence the A380 requires less runway length to take off and land. Even though it is a double-deck aircraft, it is compatible with most of the world's airport infrastructure resulting in it being able to operate safely on runways with a width of 45 metres or more (a minimum standard for most airports).

The new A380 turnaround time has been measured and validated at 90 minutes, making it fully in line with other large aircraft in use today. Because of this it can replace older and smaller wide-bodied aircraft and simultaneously provide economic and environmental gains from the same slots, being able to accommodate over 40% more passengers than

▲ *Cloudy skies await Airbus A340-600 series G-VGAS* Varga Girl *as it departs London's Heathrow Airport on 21 March 2007.* Allan Huse

aluminium, with the remaining airframe consisting of composite materials. Carbon-reinforced plastic, glass fibre-reinforced plastic and quartz fibre-reinforced plastic is used extensively in the wings, some fuselage sections, tail surface and doors. The A380 cabin noise is an impressive 50% less than a B747-400; it also has larger windows and overhead bins plus 60cm (2 feet) of extra headroom. The wider body also allows for impressive increases in seat width – seats in economy are 48cm (19 inches) wide compared to 43cm (17 inches) in a B747-400 aircraft.

Vital for any new aircraft is the issue of

▼ *An artist's impression of an Airbus A380 in Virgin Atlantic livery. Note the fictitious but apt registration code G-VXXL.* Virgin Atlantic Airways

▲ Another of Virgin Atlantic's 'appetite whetters' is this potential image of the Dreamliner flying high above the clouds. The images portraying the Dreamliners were not provided with fictitious names or registration letters.
Virgin Atlantic Airways

◀ B747-400 G-VAST Ladybird's *landing gear is captured folding away as the airliner departs Manchester for the USA in April 2007.*
Kevin Murphy

the previous largest aircraft on each flight, from the same boarding gate and slot occupancy.

Although not in Virgin Atlantic service, the first A380 to use Heathrow in May 2006 marked the official opening of the airport's Pier 6, which was specially built to accommodate new large aircraft. Interestingly 11 of the 17 likely customers (including Virgin Atlantic) have indicated that they intend to use the A380 into and out of Heathrow. Boarding the double-decker does not take any longer than the existing large aircraft, but its greater capacity will make it markedly more efficient than its rivals. Extra-wide main stairs allow boarding of passengers through the first two main deck doors without the operational need for an upper deck boarding bridge, thus resulting in swift turnarounds.

Aircraft naming

Virgin Atlantic's aircraft carry female names such as *Ladybird*, *Jersey Girl* and *Ruby Tuesday*. Many aircraft were also named after some of the airline's routes such as *Maiden Tokyo* and *California Girl*. Typical of the sense of humour associated with the Virgin brand and Sir Richard Branson are some of the fleet's registrations. *Boston Belle* G-VJFK remembered the late John F. Kennedy, whilst *Lady Penelope* G-VFAB was named after a popular character in the British children's TV show *Thunderbirds*. Virgin's first airbus, an A340-311, was 'christened' by Princess Diana as *Lady in Red* G-VBUS.

The solitary exception, being the only Virgin Atlantic aircraft to carry a male name, was *The Spirit of Sir Freddie* that was named after Branson's close friend Sir Freddie Laker. This not only reflected the esteem in which Branson held Laker but acknowledged the invaluable assistance and advice he gave when Virgin Atlantic was in its fledgling days, despite the collapse of his own airline.

G-VFAB *Lady Penelope* received a revised livery to celebrate Virgin Atlantic's 21st birthday. This involved the pin-up girl motif, first carried by G-VRED *Scarlet Lady* and designed by British artist Ken White, being moved from the front of

▼ *Boeing 747-400 series G-VFAB was renamed* Spice One *by the all-female pop group 'The Spice Girls' at Heathrow on 14 December 2007. The famous quintet's signatures were also featured on the side of the fuselage.*
Virgin Atlantic Airways

◄ *G-VFAB* Lady Penelope *departs Heathrow for distant shores on 8 October 2006. The exhaust outlet of the 'fifth engine' can be seen between the tailplanes. This engine is used to provide power for the onboard equipment when the aircraft is on the ground prior to the main engines being started up.*
Kevin Murphy

▲▲ *G-VTOP Virginia Plain takes to the skies at Manchester on 25 September 2005 en route to America. Virgin Atlantic's practice of adding a catchy phrase to the side of the fuselage is clearly seen. On this occasion first-time flyers are reminded that 'You never forget your first time'.*
Kevin Murphy

▲ *Boeing 747-400 G-VROY Pretty Woman is seen on the runway at Manchester's Ringway International Airport on 4 April 2006.*
Kevin Murphy

the fuselage to the rear and a new name added at the rear, *Birthday Girl*. Again in true Virgin fashion, a special flight numbered VS45 took to the skies with Richard Branson, several media representatives and twenty-one 21-year-olds travelling as winners of a special competition.

The B747-400 fleet has occasionally carried slogans on its fuselage sides near to the tailfins, some of these being:

'*The power of 4*' – a reference to the four engines used on the aircraft

'*You never forget your first time*' – a reference to the experience of a first flight with Virgin Atlantic

'*Backing the bid*' – showing Virgin Atlantic's support for Britain's bid to host the 2012 Olympic Games

'*Fly a younger fleet*' – a reference to the low average age of its fleet

'*No way BA/AA*' – a reference to Virgin Atlantic's objection to a proposed British Airways/American Airlines alliance.

Virgin Atlantic's aircraft have not been strangers to the silver screen either. Boeing 747-400 G-VAST *Ladybird* appeared on BBC's *Top Gear* acting as a wind source to test the strength of cars in a crosswind, whilst Airbus A340-600 G-VWIN *Lady Luck* (a very apt registration number) starred in the James Bond epic *Casino Royale* as did another A340-600 in an airport security check scene complete with Richard Branson and Virgin Atlantic crew. Interestingly the sequence represented a scene purporting to be at Miami International Airport but was filmed at Prague's Ruzyne Airport. This scene was excised from the version of *Casino Royale* that screens on British Airways flights. It is also doubtful that Virgin's reference in the latest Bond adventure, *Quantum of Solace*, will be shown uncut on British Airway's flights. It's a crucial scene to the film and if cut, the movie will not make sense to the passengers.

A full list of aircraft – giving names, construction numbers and registrations – can be found in Appendix A at the back of this book.

Manufacturer's Specifications

▲ *Boeing 747-400 G-VLIP* Hot Lips   Kevin Murphy

Boeing 747-400

Aircraft Dimensions

Wingspan	64.4 m
Overall length	70.6 m
Tail height	19.4 m
Interior cabin width	6.1 m

Basic Operating Data

Maximum passengers	386
Maximum cargo	6,025 cu ft (170.5 cu m)
Engines	Pratt & Whitney PW4062
	Rolls-Royce RB211-524H2-T
	General Electric CF6-80C2B5F
Maximum thrust	PW 63,300 lb (281.57 kN)
	RR 59,500 lb (264.67 kN)
	GE 62,100 lb (276.23 kN)
Maximum fuel capacity	216,840 litres
Maximum range	13,450 km (7,260 nm)
Typical cruise speed	0.85 Mach (913 km/h, 567 mph)
	(at 35,000 ft)

▲ *Virgin Atlantic's Dreamliner*   Virgin Atlantic Airways

Boeing 787-9 Dreamliner

Some basic facts – provided by Boeing/Virgin Atlantic:

Fuel range of between 8,000 and 8,500 nautical miles

Twin-aisle aircraft

Wingspan	203 ft (62 m)
Length	206 ft (63 m)

Expected year of entry into service – 2010

Cargo space	5,400 cu ft

The aircraft's primary structure, including the fuselage and wings, will be made of:
50% composites
20% aluminium
15% titanium
10% steel
 5% other materials

The aircraft will provide improved levels of fuel efficiency and noise emissions per seat when compared to current in-service aircraft types, making the Dreamliner quieter and more efficient

The aircraft will have advanced and innovative flight controls
Speed   Mach 0.85 (similar to a B747-400)

Days to assemble each aircraft – the goal is three days.

▲ Airbus A340-300 G-VHOL Jetstreamer — Virgin Atlantic Airways

▲ Airbus A340-600 G-VNAP Sleeping Beauty — Allan Huse

▲ Airbus A380 in Virgin Atlantic livery — Virgin Atlantic Airways

AIRBUS A340-300   A340-600

Aircraft Dimensions

	A340-300	A340-600
Overall length	63.60 m	75.30 m
Height	16.85 m	17.30 m
Fuselage diameter	5.64 m	5.64 m
Maximum cabin width	5.28 m	5.28 m
Cabin length	50.35 m	60.98 m
Wingspan (geometric)	60.30 m	63.45 m
Wing area (reference)	361.60 sq m	439.40 sq m
Wing sweep (25% chord)	30 degrees	31.10 degrees
Wheelbase	25.60 m	32.89 m
Wheel track	10.69 m	10.69 m

Basic Operating Data

Engines	CF6-80E1 or PW4000	RR Trent 500 or RR Trent 700
Engine thrust range	303 (320) kN	249 (267) kN
Typical passenger seating	240	308
Range with max passengers	10,500 km	14,360 km
Max operating Mach number	0.86 Mo	0.86 Mo
Bulk hold volume	13.76 cu m	13.76 cu m

Design Weights

Maximum ramp weight	230.9 tonnes	369.2 tonnes
Maximum take-off weight	230 tonnes	368 tonnes
Maximum landing weight	185 tonnes	259 tonnes
Maximum zero fuel weight	173 tonnes	245 tonnes
Maximum fuel capacity	97,170 litres	195,881 litres
Typical operating weight (empty)	122.2 tonnes	177.8 tonnes
Typical volumetric payload	45.9 tonnes	55.6 tonnes

AIRBUS A380-800

Aircraft Dimensions

Length	73 m (239 ft 6 in)
Span	79.8 m (261 ft 10 in)
Height	24.1 m (79 ft 1 in)
Wheelbase	30.4 m (99 ft 8 in)
Outside fuselage width	7.14 m (23 ft 6 in)
Cabin width:	
main deck	6.60 m (21 ft 8 in)
upper deck	5.94 m (19 ft 6 in)
Wing area	845 sq m (9,100 sq ft)

Basic Operating Data

Cockpit crew	2
Number of wheels	22
Seating capacity	525 (3-class)
	644 (2-class)
	853 (1-class)
Operating empty weight	276,800 kg (610,200 lbs)
Cruising speed	Mach 0.85
Maximum cruising speed	Mach 0.89
Maximum speed	Mach 0.96
Range at design load	15,200 km (8,200 nm)
Service ceiling	13,115 m (43,000 ft)
Engines (four of)	GP7270 (A380-861)
	Trent 970/B (A380-841)
	Trent 972/B (A380-842)

Design Weights

Maximum take-off weight	560,000 kg (1,235,000 lbs)
Maximum payload	90,800 kg (200,000 lbs)
Maximum fuel capacity	310,000 litres (81,900 US gallons)

Appendix A
Virgin Atlantic Fleet Overview 2008

Aircraft	In Service	Stored	Moved to Other Operator	Stored	Scrapped	Total
Airbus A320			4			4
Airbus A321			1			1
Airbus A340	25		5			30
Boeing 737			1			1
Boeing 747	13		16		2	31
Boeing 767			1			1
Total	38	0	28	0	2	68

► Caught by the camera on 15 July 2006, Virgin Atlantic's G-VROY Pretty Woman *departs Manchester en route for the USA. The proximity of the other aircraft flying nearby is evidence of the busy UK air space.* Kevin Murphy

◄ *The dark sky suggesting an impending storm is contradicted by the sunlight reflecting off G-VTOP* Virginia Plain *departing Manchester Ringway International Airport on 19 November 2006.* Kevin Murphy

Aircraft Registration	Aircraft Type	Name	Year Built	Entered Service with VAA	Seating Arrangement U/C, P/E, E/C *
G-VFAB	B747-400	Lady Penelope Birthday Girl Spice One	1994	1994	54 / 62 / 228
G-VHOT	B747-400	Tubular Belle	1994	1994	54 / 62 / 228
G-VBIG	B747-400	Tinkerbelle	1996	1996	54 / 62 / 228
G-VTOP	B747-400	Virginia Plain	1996	1997	14 / 58 / 380
G-VAIR	A340-300	Maiden Tokyo	1997	1997	34 / 35 / 171
G-VSEA	A340-300	Plain Sailing	1992	1997	34 / 35 / 171
G-VHOL	A340-300	Jetstreamer	1992	1997	34 / 35 / 171
G-VAST	B747-400	Ladybird	1997	1997	14 / 58 / 380
G-VELD	A340-300	African Queen	1997	1998	34 / 35 / 171
G-VFAR	A340-300	Diana	1998	1998	34 / 35 / 171
G-VXLG	B747-400	Ruby Tuesday	1998	1998	14 / 58 / 380
G-VROS	B747-400	English Rose	2001	2001	14 / 58 / 379
G-VGAL	B747-400	Jersey Girl	2001	2001	14 / 58 / 379
G-VLIP	B747-400	Hot Lips	2001	2001	14 / 58 / 379
G-VROM	B747-400	Barbarella	2001	2001	14 / 58 / 379
G-VROY	B747-400	Pretty Woman	2001	2001	14 / 58 / 379
G-VWOW	B747-400	Cosmic Girl	2001	2001	54 / 62 / 228
G-VSHY	A340-642	Madam Butterfly Claudia Nine	2002	2002	45 / 38 / 225
G-VMEG	A340-600	Mystic Maiden	2002	2002	45 / 38 / 225
G-VOGE	A340-642	Cover Girl	2002	2002	45 / 38 / 225
G-VFOX	A340-600	Silver Lady	2002	2002	45 / 38 / 225
G-VGOA	A340-600	Indian Princess	2003	2003	45 / 38 / 225
G-VATL	A340-600	Miss Kitty Atlantic Angel	2003	2003	45 / 38 / 225
G-VROC	B747-400	Mustang Sally	2003	2003	54 / 62 / 228
G-VEIL	A340-600	Queen of the Skies	2004	2004	45 / 38 / 225
G-VSSH	A340-600	Sweet Dreamer	2005	2005	45 / 38 / 225
G-VNAP	A340-600	Sleeping Beauty	2005	2005	45 / 38 / 225
G-VGAS	A340-600	Varga Girl	2005	2005	45 / 38 / 225
G-VWKD	A340-600	Miss Behavin	2005	2005	45 / 38 / 225
G-VBLU	A340-600	Soul Sister	2006	2006	45 / 38 / 225
G-VWIN	A340-600	Lady Luck	2006	2006	45 / 38 / 225
G-VFIT	A340-600	Dancing Queen	2006	2006	45 / 38 / 225
G-VFIZ	A340-600	Bubbles	2006	2006	45 / 38 / 225
G-VYOU	A340-600	Emmeline Heaney	2006	2006	45 / 38 / 225
G-VRED	A340-600	Scarlet Lady	2006	2006	45 / 38 / 225
G-VWEB	A340-600	Surfer Girl	2006	2006	45 / 38 / 225
G-VSUN	A340-300	Little Miss Sunshine Rainbow Lady	1996	2007	34 / 35 / 171
G-VBUG	A340-600	Lady Bird	2007	2007	45 / 38 / 225

*U/C = Upper Class, P/E = Premium Economy, E/C = Economy Class

▶ New in 2006 is Airbus A340-600 G-VRED *Scarlet Lady, seen on the ground at Heathrow Airport.*
Allan Huse

Ex-Virgin Atlantic Fleet (2008)

Aircraft	Construction Number	Registration	Year Built	Delivery to VAA	Disposal
747-287B	21189	G-VIRG *Maiden Voyager*	1976	14/06/84	12/2001 as 5N-NNN to Kabo Air
747-243B	19732	G-VGIN	1971	31/10/86	10/2001 as 5N-EEE to Kabo Air
747-212B	21939	G-TKYO	1980	31/03/89	12/1994 as N616FF to Tower Air
747-212B	21937	G-VRGN	1980	27/08/89	02/1995 as N618FF to Tower Air
747-283B	20121	G-VOYG	1971	03/02/90	Aircraft scrapped
747-123	20108	G-VMIA	1970	22/03/90	Aircraft scrapped
747-238B	20842	G-VJFK	1974	02/02/91	07/2001 as 5N-PDP to Kabo Air
747-206B	20427	PH-BUG	1971	15/04/91	05/1991 as PH-BUG to Garuda
747-238B	20921	G-VLAX *California Girl* *Honey Pie*	1974	01/05/91	07/2001 as 5N-PPP to Kabo Air
A340-311	13	G-VBUS *Lady in Red*	1993	26/11/93	06/2005 as G-VBUS to Virgin Nigeria Airways
A340-311	15	G-VAEL *Maiden Toulouse*	1993	15/12/93	01/2007 as EC-KAJ to Air Comet
A340-311	16	G-VSKY *China Girl*	1994	21/10/94	01/2004 as 9Y-JIL to BWIA
A340-311	58	G-VFLY *Dragon Lady*	1994	24/10/94	06/2006 as OH-LQA to Finnair
A320-321	429	EI-TLE	1993	14/02/95	06/1995 as EI-TLE to Translift Airways
A320-211	449	EI-VIR	1993	08/04/95	11/1995 as G-OUZO to All Leisure Airways
A320-211	449	G-OUZO	1993	01/04/96	04/2000 as G-JOEM to Airtours
A340-313	114	G-VSUN *Rainbow Lady*	1996	30/04/96	04/2006 as G-VSUN to Virgin Nigeria Airways
767-31AER	24428	PH-MCG	1989	22/09/96	03/1997 as PH-MCG to Martinair Holland
747-267B	22872	G-VCAT	1982	15/10/98	12/2001 as TF-ATK to Air Atlanta Icelandic

Aircraft	Construction Number	Registration	Year Built	Delivery to VAA	Disposal
747-267B	23048	G-VRUM	1983	31/10/98	12/2001 as TF-ATV to Air Atlanta Icelandic
747-219B	22723	G-VBEE	1981	05/04/99	12/2000 as TF-ATN to Air Atlanta Icelandic
747-219B	22722	G-VZZZ	1981	07/07/99	03/2005 as VP-BQE to Transaero Airlines
747-219B	22791	G-VIBE	1982	25/09/99	06/2005 as VP-BQH to Transaero Airlines
747-219B	22725	G-VPUF	1982	22/03/00	10/2006 as VP-BQC to Transaero Airlines
A321-211	1219	G-VATH	2000	12/05/00	02/2003 as EC-IMA to LTE
747-219B	22724	G-VSSS *Island Lady*	1981	23/05/00	01/2002 as TF-ATW to Air Atlanta Icelandic
747-267B	22530	TF-ABA	1981	16/01/01	01/2003 as TF-ABA to Air Atlanta Icelandic
747-267B	23048	G-VRUM	1983	09/04/02	01/2004 as G-CCMB to European Air Charter
747-267B	22872	G-VCAT	1982	19/04/02	12/2003 as G-CCMA to European Air Charter
747-219B	22723	TF-ATN	1981	24/06/02	04/2004 returned to Virgin Atlantic as G-VBEE
A320-214	978	G-VMED	1999	15/10/03	04/2004 as TC-OGF to Atlas Jet
747-219B	22723	G-VBEE	1981	14/04/04	02/2005 as P4-TSO to Transaero Airlines

▼ *The Virgin Atlantic livery is worn to good effect by the airline's fleet as can be seen in this photograph of A340-600 G-VGAS* Varga Girl, *which shows off the underbelly detail and sleek profile of the aircraft.*
Azizul M. Islam

▲ *The under-wing profile and detail are well shown in this photograph of Airbus A340-600 G-VSSH* Sweet Dreamer.
Darren Varney

VIRGIN NIGERIA FLEET (2008)

ACTIVE FLEET (2008)

Aircraft	Construction Number	Registration	Year Built	Delivery to VNA	Origin
A320-211	294	LZ-BHB	1992	17/08/06	As LZ-BHB from BH Air (Balkan Holidays)
A340-313	114	G-VSUN *Rainbow Lady*	1996	12/04/06	As G-VSUN from Virgin Atlantic
737-33V	29337	5N-VND	1999	20/06/06	As G-EZYM from EasyJet
737-33V	29338	5N-VNC	1999	05/04/06	As G-EZYN from EasyJet
737-33V	29340	5N-VNE	1999	07/10/06	As G-EZYP from EasyJet
737-33V	29341	5N-VNF	1999	27/11/06	As G-EZYR from EasyJet
737-33V	29342	5N-VNG	1999	10/12/06	As G-EZYS from EasyJet
767-3Y0	24952	YL-LCY	1991	27/04/07	As YL-LCY from LAT Charter Airlines
767-3Y0	25000	YL-LCZ	1991	22/06/07	As C-GHPA from Air Canada Fokker
F-27-050	20233	PH-JXK	1991	01/03/07	As PH-JXK from Denim Air

▶ *Seen on 10 November 2005 is Virgin Nigeria Airbus A340-311 G-VBUS, formerly Virgin Atlantic Lady in Red, transferred to its new employer in June 2005 but still carrying its previous owner's registration code.*
Linda Chen

▲ *Formerly Virgin Nigeria's G-WWBD, Airbus A330-243 is seen still carrying the Virgin logo on its tailfin at Gatwick Airport on 16 February 2007.*
Allan Huse

▶ *Airbus A320-211 LZ-BHB of the Virgin Nigeria fleet is seen on 15 June 2006 stored at Brussels, Belgium, awaiting delivery of a replacement engine.*
Koos Van Der Heijden

Ex-Virgin Nigeria Fleet (2008)

Aircraft	Construction Number	Registration	Year Built	Delivery to VNA	Disposal
A320-211	221	LZ-BHD	1991	20/04/05	08/2006 as LZ-BHD to BH Air (Balkan Holidays)
A320-211	294	LZ-BHB	1992	01/05/05	04/2006 as LZ-BHB to BH Air (Balkan Holidays)
A330-243	401	G-WWBD	2001	28/01/07	05/2007 to bmi British Midland as G-WWBD
A340-311	13	G-VBUS *Lady in Red*	1993	10/06/05	03/2007 as EC-KCF to Air Comet
737-36N	28563	N306FL	1997	23/10/05	05/2007 as HZ-NMA to SAMA
737-33V	29339	5N-VNB	1999	24/03/06	08/2007 as LN-KKD to Norwegian Air Shuttle

Some interesting facts about Virgin Atlantic Airways

Number of employees worldwide	8,900
Number of pilots	700
Number of cabin crew	4,000
Passengers carried 1984-2008	63.5 million
Classes of travel	Upper Class Premium Economy Economy
Aircraft types (2007)	Boeing 747-400 Airbus A340-600 Airbus A340-300
Future aircraft type on order	Boeing 787-9 Dreamliners Airbus A380 (order options)

Financial Statistics

Year Ended	Turnover £m	Profit (Loss) Pre-Tax £m
31 July 1989	106.8	8.4
31 July 1990	208.8	8.7
31 October 1991 (15 months)	382.9	6.2
31 October 1992	356.9	(14.5)
31 October 1993	400.9	0.5
31 October 1994	503.4	(3.0)
31 August 1995 (10 months)	507.0	36.5
30 April 1996 (8 months)	440.0	41.3
30 April 1997	785.1	64.7
30 April 1998	942.3	91.2
30 April 1999	1,066.6	98.7
30 April 2000	1,267.6	4.1
30 April 2001	1,517.5	45.5
30 April 2002	1,499.8	(92.6)
30 April 2003	1,401.2	15.7
29 February 2004 (10 months)	1,272.0	20.9
28 February 2005*	1,630.0	20.1
28 February 2006*	1,912.3	41.6
28 February 2007	2,141.4	46.8**
29 February 2008	2,336.0	60.9

* pre-tax profit, pre-exceptional items
** excluding Virgin Nigeria

VIRGIN ATLANTIC ROUTE NETWORK

Route	Flight Numbers
United States of America	
Heathrow / New York (Newark) / Heathrow (two services per day)	VS001-VS002, VS017-VS018
Heathrow / New York (JFK) / Heathrow (four services per day)	VS003-VS004, VS009-VS010, VS045-VS046, VS025-VS026
Heathrow / Miami / Heathrow	VS005-VS006
Heathrow / Los Angeles / Heathrow (two services per day)	VS007-VS008, VS023-VS024
Heathrow / Boston / Heathrow	VS011-VS012
Heathrow / San Francisco / Heathrow	VS019-VS020
Heathrow / Washington DC / Heathrow (two services per day)	VS021-VS022, VS055-VS056
Heathrow / Chicago / Heathrow	VS039-VS040
Gatwick / Orlando / Gatwick (two services per day)	VS015-VS016, VS027-VS028
Gatwick / Las Vegas / Gatwick	VS043-VS044
Manchester / Orlando / Manchester	VS075-VS076
Africa	
Heathrow / Johannesburg / Heathrow	VS601-VS602
Heathrow / Cape Town / Heathrow	VS603-VS604
Heathrow / Lagos / Heathrow	VS651-VS652
Heathrow / Nairobi / Heathrow	VS671-VS672
Asia Pacific	
Heathrow / Tokyo / Heathrow	VS900-VS901
Heathrow / Hong Kong /Sydney / Hong Kong / Heathrow	VS200-VS201
Heathrow / Shanghai / Heathrow	VS250-VS251
Heathrow / Delhi / Heathrow	VS300-VS301
Heathrow / Mumbai / Heathrow	VS350-VS351
Indian	
Heathrow / Mauritius / Heathrow	VS372-VS373
Middle East	
Heathrow / Dubai / Heathrow	VS400-VS401
Caribbean	
Gatwick / Kingston / Gatwick	VS069-VS070
Gatwick / Barbados / Gatwick	VS029-VS030
Gatwick / St Lucia / Gatwick	VS031-VS032
Gatwick / Antigua / Gatwick	VS033-VS034
Gatwick / Tobago / Grenada / Tobago / Gatwick	VS051-VS052
Gatwick / Havana / Gatwick	VS063-VS064
Gatwick / Montego Bay / Gatwick	VS065-VS066
Manchester / Barbados / Manchester	VS077-VS078
Manchester / St Lucia / Manchester	VS079-VS080

VIRGIN ATLANTIC PASSENGERS CARRIED YEAR BY YEAR

Year	Annual	Cumulative
1984	124,711	124,711
1985	245,404	370,115
1986	289,060	659,175
1987	464,196	1,123,371
1988	626,319	1,749,690
1989	619,506	2,369,196
1990	837,136	3,206,332
1991	1,044,760	4,251,092
1992	1,239,011	5,490,103
1993	1,398,834	6,888,937
1994	1,679,403	8,568,340
1995	2,029,624	10,597,964
1996	2,293,802	12,891,766
1997	2,806,538	15,698,304
1998	3,206,117	18,904,421
1999	3,622,422	22,526,843
2000	4,280,044	26,806,887
2001	4,105,115	30,912,002
2002	3,808,687	34,720,689
2003	3,850,578	38,571,267
2004	4,323,268	42,891,554
2005	4,483,262	47,374,816
2006	5,142,080	52,516,896
2007	5,921,766	58,438,662

VIRGIN ATLANTIC PASSENGERS 5 YEARLY COMPARISON TO/FROM THE UK

TOTAL PASSENGER NUMBERS:

	1985	1990	1995	2000	2005	2006	2007
London							
New York	213,348	354,445	532,170	1,039,866	899,765	917,542	1,032,086
Florida	0	287,543	491,223	984,957	723,861	655,321	687,903
East Coast	0	0	215,546	456,761	314,114	331,946	447,934
West Coast	0	122,933	427,787	735,038	760,842	834,849	891,267
Caribbean	0	0	0	229,614	475,869	563,132	650,644
Nigeria	0	0	0	0	200,314	139,864	158,328
South Africa	0	0	0	191,814	190,040	235,762	274,873
India	0	0	0	23,942	176,022	251,396	296,569
China	0	0	135,018	204,063	272,417	257,781	266,689
Japan	0	72,215	127,505	148,547	143,101	151,041	156,719
Sydney	0	0	0	0	32,440	60,793	76,208
Dubai	0	0	0	0	0	108,265	170,308
Kenya	0	0	0	0	0	0	63,969
Mauritius	0	0	0	0	0	0	7,476
Manchester							
Orlando	0	0	0	176,161	239,403	254,286	328,896
Barbados	0	0	0	0	2,284	31,981	33,167
St Lucia	0	0	0	0	0	2,577	10,773

MARKET SHARE %

Route	2003	2004	2005	2006	2007
London to/from					
New York	24	25	24	20.1	20.9
Florida	47	48	48	53.1	56.6
East Coast	19	21	17	16.8	19
West Coast	25	26	32	31.5	32.2
Caribbean	55	59	57	57.6	58.7
Nigeria	46	52	53	32.1	32.3
South Africa	15	13	13	15.5	17.3
India	18	23	18	15.9	17.8
China	22	22	8	7.9	8.2
Japan	15	16	15	17.3	18.5
Sydney			24	23.2	24.3
Manchester to/from					
Orlando			96	37.3	100
Barbados			6	10.6	44
St Lucia					100

Virgin Atlantic Cargo –
Performance Statistics

Tonnage (Comparison Year on Year)

Year Ended	Tonnage Carried
April 1997	88,452
April 1998	112,751
April 1999	113,649
April 2000	134,453
April 2001	142,639
April 2002	124,408
April 2003	126,670
February 2004 (10 months)	113,609
February 2005	149,492
February 2006	163,165
February 2007	188,147
February 2008	211,570

Route Revenue Contribution

Cumulative – Year ended February 2008

Route	Contribution %
New York	11
Florida	7
West Coast	12
East Coast	7
Caribbean	2
Far East	44
Africa including Middle East and Mauritius	17

AWARDS WON
BY VIRGIN ATLANTIC

2008

Skytrax World Awards	Heathrow – Best Business Class Lounge
Red Dot Awards	Hall of Fame – Design Excellence
Rough Guides	Most Child Friendly Airline
Business Travel Awards	Best Long-haul Business Airline
Globe Travel Awards	Best Scheduled Airline to USA/Canada Favourite Airline

2007

World Travel Awards US	World's Leading Airport Lounge
Zagat's Global Airline	Best Frequent Flyer Programme in the World Survey
Travel & Leisure's Global Vision Awards US	Corporative Initiative for Environmental Work
Business Travel Awards	Airline of the Year
	Best Airline – Economy
	Best Airline – Business
	Best Scheduled Airline, Long-haul
	Favourite Scheduled Airline, Long-haul
	Best Customer Service for an Airline
Business Traveller	Best Business Class
	Best Premium Economy
Travel Trade Gazette	Best Business Airline
Conde Nast Reader Travel Awards	Best Leisure Airline, Long-haul
Red Dot Awards	Product Design – Heathrow Clubhouse
D&AD Awards	Environmental Design – Heathrow Clubhouse
Jet Set Airline Awards US	eCityofStyle2007 Jet Set Airline Award
Lighting Design Awards	Isometrix Lighting and Design for the London Heathrow Clubhouse
Design Week Awards	Best of Show – Heathrow Clubhouse
	Hospitality Environmental – Heathrow Clubhouse
Travel Weekly's Readers Choice Awards US	Best International Airline
Travel Weekly Globe Awards	Best Scheduled Airline to USA/Canada
TTG Business Travel People Awards	Best Sales Team

2006

Buying Business Travel Diamond Awards	Best Business Airline
	Best Transatlantic Airline
FX Design Award	Winner – Best Leisure or Entertainment Venue
Campaign Poster Awards	Five awards for Advertising
Group Leisure Magazine	Best Airline for Groups
TTG Awards	Business Airline of the Year
Business Traveller	Best Business Class
	Best Premium Economy
Conde Nast Traveller	Top Business Class on Transatlantic routes
BACA 'Excellence'	Best Passenger Airline
Business Travel World	Best Long-haul Business Airline

Air Cargo News	Cargo Airline of the Year
	Best Cargo Airline to North America
Air Cargo World	Award for Excellence
Forbes	Best Business Class
Skytrax World Awards	World's Best Business Class Lounge
North American Travel Journalism Association	Best Foreign Airline

2005

DBA Design Effectiveness Awards	Industrial product – Upper Class Suite
Business Traveller	Best Premium Economy Class
New Media Age Effectiveness Awards	Travel Category, Virgin Atlantic Website Redesign
Lighting Design Awards	Transport Lighting – Upper Class Suite
Air Transport World	Passenger Service Award
International Forum (IF) Design Awards	IF Product Design – Upper Class Suite
Air Cargo News	Best Cargo Airline to North America
Air Carrier – Air Cargo World	Award for Excellence

2004

Wallpaper Design Awards	Most Life Enhancing Item – Upper Class Suite
BSME Awards	Editor of The Year – Michael Jacovides for *Carlos*
TTG Awards	Best Long-haul Scheduled Airline
Travel Bulletin Awards	Top Leisure Scheduled Airline
Business Traveller	Best Premium Economy Class
Magazine Design	Best Design Magazine of The Year – *Carlos*
	Best Use of Illustration – *Carlos*
	Best Designed Customer Magazine – *Carlos*
IDEA Awards	Gold Award – Transport Design, Upper Class Suite
Red Dot Awards	Best of the Best High Quality Design – Upper Class Suite Interior
	Best High Quality Design – Upper Class Suite
ID Annual Review	Best in Furniture – Upper Class Suite
Group Travel Awards	Best Airline for Groups
The Design and Art Direction Awards	Transport Product Design – Upper Class Suite
The Guardian Travel	Best Business Airline
Communicators in Business Awards	Internal Online Publications – Verb Online
Design Week	Industrial Product Design Winner – Upper Class Suite
	Editorial Design Winner – Carlos
Business Travel	Best Long-haul Business Airline
Travel Weekly	Best Transatlantic Airline
Recruitment Advertising Awards	Graduate/Trainee – Engineering Apprenticeships
	General Appointments – Hairdressers' Adverts
	Hospitality/Travel/Leisure – IFBT Adverts
Air Cargo News	Best Cargo Airline to North America
	Best Cargo Airline to The Far East

VIRGIN BLUE FLEET (2008)

Note: Virgin Atlantic has no shareholding in Virgin Blue Airlines, although its parent company Virgin Group is a minority shareholder. In view of this, the Virgin Blue Airlines fleet list has been included here for information purposes only.

ACTIVE FLEET (2008):

Aircraft	Construction Number	Registration	Year Built	Delivery to VBA	Name
737-7Q8	28238	VH-VBA	2001	27/04/01	*Brizzie Lizzie*
737-7Q8	28240	VH-VBB	2001	03/05/01	*Barossa Babe*
737-86N	28644	VH-VOG	2001	05/12/01	*Misty Blue*
737-86N	29884	VH-VOH	2002	22/03/02	*Jazzy Blue*
737-76Q	30288	VH-VBU	2003	15/05/03	*Darwin Diva*
737-8BK	30620	VH-VOA	2001	06/11/01	*Blue Belle*
737-8BK	30622	VH-VOB	2002	15/04/02	*Matilda Blue*
737-8BK	30623	VH-VOC	2002	22/05/02	*Skye Blue*
737-8BK	30624	VH-VOD	2002	14/08/02	*Blue Moon*
737-7Q8	30630	VH-VBF	2001	17/12/01	*Mellie Melbourne*
737-7Q8	30633	VH-VBL	2002	15/10/02	*Victoria Vixen*
737-7Q8	30638	VH-VBC	2001	05/06/01	*Betty Blue*
737-7Q8	30641	VH-VBH	2002	01/03/02	*Spirit of Salty*
737-7Q8	30644	VH-VBI	2002	11/04/02	*Smurfette*
737-7Q8	30647	VH-VBJ	2002	21/06/02	*Perth Princess*
737-7Q8	30648	VH-VBK	2002	11/07/02	*Lady Victoria*
737-7Q8	30658	VH-VOV	2003	22/05/03	*Alluring Alice*
737-7Q8	30665	VH-VOU	2004	30/01/04	*Blue Billie*
737-7Q8	30707	VH-VBD	2001	17/10/01	*Sassy Sydney*
737-7BX	30740	VH-VBT	2001	31/01/03	*Launie Lass*
737-7BX	30743	VH-VBP	2002	06/09/02	*Déjà Blue*
737-7BX	30744	VH-VBQ	2002	13/09/02	*La Blue Femme*
737-7BX	30745	VH-VBR	2002	09/09/02	*Mackay Maiden*
737-7BX	30746	VH-VBS	2002	16/09/02	*Blue Baroness*
737-76N	32734	VH-VBM	2002	21/03/02	*Tassie Tigress*
737-8Q8	32798	VH-VOW	2004	25/03/04	*Jillaroo Blue*
737-76N	33005	VH-VBN	2002	27/06/02	*Southern Belle*
737-7BK	33015	VH-VBV	2003	10/10/03	*Moulin Blue*
737-8BK	33017	VH-VOX	2004	18/02/05	*Brindabella Blue*
737-76N	33418	VH-VBO	2002	08/11/02	*Tropical Temptress*
737-8FE	33758	VH-VOK	2003	13/08/03	*Smoochy Maroochy*
737-8FE	33759	VH-VOL	2003	20/08/03	*Goldie Coast*
737-8FE	33794	VH-VOM	2003	12/09/03	*Little Blue Peep*

Aircraft	Construction Number	Registration	Year Built	Delivery to VBA	Name
737-8FE	33795	VH-VON	2003	11/09/03	*Scarlet Blue*
737-8FE	33798	VH-VOQ	2003	01/10/03	*Peter Pan*
737-8FE	33800	VH-VOS	2004	14/06/04	*Kimberley Cutie*
737-8FE	33801	VH-VOT	2004	31/05/04	*Butterfly Blue*
737-8FE	33997	VH-VUA	2004	27/08/04	*Virginia Blue*
737-8FE	34013	VH-VUB	2004	21/09/04	*Billie Blue*
737-8FE	34014	VH-VUC	2004	14/10/04	*Foxy Rock'sy*
737-8FE	34015	VH-VUD	2004	04/11/04	*Bewitching Broome*
737-8FE	34167	VH-VUE	2005	02/04/05	*Prue Blue*
737-8FE	34168	VH-VUF	2005	29/04/05	*Hobart Honey*
737-7FE	34322	VH-VBZ	2005	01/09/05	*Matilda*
737-7FE	34323	VH-VBY	2005	28/07/05	*Virgin-ia Blue* (airline's 50th plane; carrying blue livery)
737-8FE	34438	VH-VUG	2006	25/05/06	*Jasmine Tasman*
737-8FE	34440	VH-VUH	2006	31/07/06	*Lady Rebecca*
737-8FE	34441	VH-VUI	2006	11/08/06	*Brandi Blue*
737-8FE	34443	VH-VUJ	2006	27/09/06	*Suzie Blue*

Ex-Virgin Blue Airlines Fleet (2008)

Aircraft	Construction Number	Registration	Year Built	Delivery to VBA	Disposal
737-4YO	23980	VH-VGD	1989	01/12/00	05/2002 as OO-VJO to Virgin Express
737-33A	24461	VH-CZQ	1990	29/10/01	03/2004 as UR-VVI to Aerosvit Airlines
737-4Q8	25740	VH-VGB	1993	31/08/00	05/2005 as EI-CZG to Air One
737-4Q8	26302	VH-VOZ	1994	01/06/00	05/2002 as EI-CXM to Air One
737-43Q	28489	VH-VGA	1996	29/05/00	05/2002 as OO-VEP to Virgin Express
737-43Q	28493	VH-VGE	1996	15/02/01	02/2003 as OO-VES to Virgin Express
737-46M	28549	VH-VGC	1997	17/11/00	03/2002 as OO-VEC to Virgin Express
737-705	29091	VH-VBW	1999	15/07/03	11/2004 as B-5091 to Changan Airlines
737-705	29092	VH-VBX	1999	23/07/03	11/2004 as B-5092 to Changan Airlines
737-86Q	30272	VH-VOE	2001	07/12/01	02/2005 as TC-SUO to Sun Express
737-86Q	30274	VH-VOF	2001	05/12/01	04/2005 as TC-SUU to Sun Express
737-81Q	30786	VH-VOI	2002	28/05/02	09/2006 as B-5156 to China Southern Airlines
737-81Q	30787	VH-VOJ	2002	22/11/02	02/2007 as B-5157 to China Southern Airlines
737-8FE	33796	VH-VOO	2003	16/09/03	01/2004 as ZK-PBA to Pacific Blue
737-8FE	33797	VH-VOP	2003	02/10/03	01/2005 as ZK-PBB to Pacific Blue
737-8FE	33799	VH-VOR	2004	16/04/04	11/2005 as ZK-PBF to Polynesian Blue

VIRGIN AMERICA FLEET (2008)

Note: Virgin Atlantic has no shareholding in Virgin America Airlines, although its parent company Virgin Group is a minority shareholder. In view of this, the Virgin America Airways fleet list has been included here for information purposes only.

Active Fleet (2008):

Aircraft	Construction	Registration Number	Year Built	Delivery to VAmA	Comment
A319-112	3181	N523VA	2007	10/07/07	Brand new
A320-214	2616	N621VA	2006	24/02/06	Brand new
A320-214	2674	N622VA	2006	25/03/06	Brand new
A320-214	2800	N625VA	2006	20/06/06	Brand new
A320-214	2830	N626VA	2006	11/07/06	Brand new
A320-214	2851	N627VA	2006	25/08/06	Brand new
A320-214	2993	N628VA	2007	19/01/07	Brand new
A320-214	3101	N630VA	2007	28/04/07	Brand new
A320-214	3135	N631VA	2007	26/05/07	Brand new
A320-214	3155	N632VA	2007	12/06/07	Brand new

Ex-Virgin America Fleet (2008)

Aircraft	Construction	Registration Number	Year Built	Delivery to VAmA	Disposal
A320-214	2778	N624VA	2006	31/05/06	Stored
A319-112	2773	N521VA	2006	16/05/06	12/2006 as N521VA to Skybus
A319-112	2811	N522VA	2006	29/06/06	02/2007 as N522VA to Skybus
A320-214	2740	N623VA	2006	03/05/06	05/2007 as PR-MHH to TAM
A320-214	3037	N629VA	2007	23/02/07	05/2007 as PR-MHL to TAM

◀ *Brand new, with her fuselage showing she was 'Air - born 2007' and carrying yet another very apt registration number is Airbus A340-600 G-VFIT* Dancing Queen.
Darren Varney

▼ *B747-400 G-VAST* Ladybird *is seen at Manchester's Ringway International Airport, reminding onlookers of* 'The power of 4'.
Kevin Murphy

BIBLIOGRAPHY

Aerospace Technology
www.aerospace-
    technology.com/projects/a340-200/
08/05/2008

Aviation Explorer
www.aviationexplorer.com/a340_facts.htm
08/05/2008

Boeing 747
http://en.wikipedia.org/wiki/Boeing_747
08/05/2008

Branson, R.
Losing My Virginity
Virgin Publishing Ltd, 1998

Conway, Richard and Tizzard, Paul
*Flying Without Fear: 101 Fear of Flying
    Questions Answered*
Betchworth: Flying Without Fear
    Publications, 2008

Flying Without Fear Ltd website
www.flyingwithoutfear.info/
15/04/2008

Gregory, Martyn
*Dirty Tricks: British Airways' Secret War
    Against Virgin Atlantic*
Warner Books, 1996

Virgin Atlantic
Press Information Kit 2007 and 2008

Virgin Atlantic Airways
Wikipedia 2007

Virgin Atlantic Website
www.virgin-atlantic.com
11/09/2007

Virgin Nigeria Airways
www.virginnigeria.com
10/04/2008

ACKNOWLEDGEMENTS

Airbus UK

www.airbus.com

www.airfleets.net

Balmforth, Jennifer

Balmforth, Linda

Balmforth, Shirley

Boeing, Seattle

Branson, Sir Richard

Caddy, Alun J.

Charles, Paul – Director of Communications,
    Virgin Atlantic

Conway, Richard – Virgin Atlantic Flying
    Without Fear Ltd

Francis, Katie – Virgin Atlantic

Hogan, Cllr Paul

Knowles, Anna – Virgin Atlantic Press Office

Legge, Jenny – Virgin Atlantic Cabin Crew
    (Flying Without Fear Course)

O'Hare, Steve

www.planespotters.net

Ridgway, Steve CBE – Chief Executive, Virgin
    Atlantic

Rowe, Jim

Tizzard, Paul – Flying Without Fear Ltd

Virgin Blue

Virgin Trains

Whitehorn, Will – Virgin Group

Glossary

AA	American Airlines		PanAm	Pan American
ACARS	Aircraft Communications Addressing and Reporting System		TCAS	Traffic Collision Avoidance System
AED	Automatic External Defibrillators		TTG	Travel Trade Gazette
ANA	All Nippon Airways		TWA	Trans World Airlines
BA	British Airways		UK	United Kingdom
BAA	British Airports Authority		UNICEF	United Nations Children's Fund (formerly United Nations International Children's Emergency Fund)
BACA	Baltic Air Charter Association			
B-Cal	British Caledonian		USA	United States of America
BSME	British Society of Magazine Editors		USDOT	United States Department of Transportation
BWIA	British West Indian Airways			
CAA	Civil Aviation Authority		VAA	Virgin Atlantic Airways
CIDA	Community and Individual Development Association		VAmA	Virgin America Airways
			VBA	Virgin Blue Airways
D&AD	The Design and Art Direction Awards		VNA	Virgin Nigeria Airways
DBA	Design Business Association			
DfT	Department for Transport			
ECAM	Electronic Centralised Aircraft Monitor			
EFIS	Electronic Flight Instrument System			
FAA	Federal Aviation Administration			
FANS A	Forward Air Navigator System			
ft	Feet (Imperial measurement)			
FWF	Flying Without Fear Ltd			
FX	FX International Interior Design			
GPS	Global Positioning System			
GPWS	Ground Proximity Warning System			
HRH	Her Royal Highness			
IDEA	Innovation and Design Excellence			
IF	International Forum			
IFBT	Inflight Beauty Therapist			
JFK	John F. Kennedy			
km	Kilometres			
kN	Nautical kilometres			
LED	Light Emitting Diode			
LTE	LTE International Airways			
MLS	Microwave Landing System			
MTOW	Maximum Take-Off Weight			
nm	Nautical miles			

The Virgin Unite Charity: Richard Branson School of Entrepreneurship

Virgin Unite is the not-for-profit entrepreneurial foundation of the Virgin Group. It works with partners from all over the world to develop new approaches to social and environmental issues. The charity is fortunate that Sir Richard Branson and the Virgin Group pick up its overhead costs so that 100% of all donations received go directly to the frontline where funding is needed most. Virgin Unite believes that the only way we are going to drive the scale of change that needs to happen in the world is if we revolutionise the way that businesses and the social sector work together. It wants to use the entrepreneurial energy across the Virgin Group to help drive this revolution.

The Branson School of Entrepreneurship was launched in October 2005 when Virgin Unite teamed up with social entrepreneur Taddy Bletcher, founder of CIDA, South Africa's first virtually-free university, to create the school and help:

■ Develop potential entrepreneurs in a practical, relevant and holistic way

■ Provide students with real-world business skills and mentorship

■ Promote entrepreneurship as a desirable career option, and

■ Support start-ups and micro-enterprises with skills, mentors, services, networks and finance arrangements.

At the school, students' business plans are prepared for launch upon graduation and they are provided with a virtual office, with a desk, computer, telephone, Internet access, as well as a meeting room with boardroom facilities. The school creates business opportunities that help student entrepreneurs follow their dreams of owning and managing successful businesses. With the right support and management the Branson School is helping future entrepreneurs make a huge difference not only to themselves but also to their families, communities and ultimately the whole of South Africa.

If you wish to make a donation to the Virgin Unite Foundation, or have any questions about its work, the charity can be contacted as follows:

By post: Virgin Unite
The School House
50 Brook Green
Hammersmith
London, W6 7BJ

By email: contact@virginunite.co.uk

Website: www.virginunite.co.uk

All of the author's royalties from the sale of this book are being donated to The Richard Branson School of Entrepreneurship section of the Virgin Unite Charity.

▲ *Virgin Atlantic's Airbus A340-600 G-VMEG* Mystic Maiden *takes to the skies at sunset.*
Sascha Kamrau